D1449175

THE SOCIAL CONTEXT OF RELIGIOSITY

Jerry D. Cardwell
Longwood College

BIP87

University Press
of America™

For Nancy, my wife, and Robert
and Jonathon, my sons, who
are the three most important
dimensions of my life.

ACKNOWLEDGEMENTS

Special thanks must be given to Dr. Glenn M. Vernon of the University of Utah. Dr. Vernon has been and continues to be an important dimension of my theoretical and research interests in the sociology of religiosity. His influence is present throughout this book.

Ms. Bonnie Gheen, our departmental student assistant, spent many hours working on the unpleasant details of putting the book together which has earned her my deepest gratitude.

I would also like to extend my real appreciation to Mrs. Peggy Golubic, our departmental secretary. This is an important part of this acknowledgment page, because it is certain that without her dedication to task and peculiar expertise, this book would not have been possible. Thank you, Peggy!

Professor James G. Silliman, Jr., Department of Education and Psychology, Longwood College, provided the photograph of Johns Memorial Episcopal Church on page xi.

The author wishes to express his thanks to the following professional journals for permission to reprint his works:

1. The Pacific Sociological Review

2. Sociological Analysis

3. Measuring Mormonism

4. The Virginia Social Science Journal

TABLE OF CONTENTS

PREFACE

Prior to 1960 the conceptual, theoretical, and empirical status of the sociological notion of religiosity could best be characterized as stagnant. Although sociologists expressed a continuing interest in the concept of religiosity in their research, the sophistication relative to its theoretical development and empirical measurement remained at a level representative of sociology in the 1940's and 1950's. During this period religiosity was understood to be an important variable in the sociology of religion but its theoretical meaning was taken as implicitly understood without benefit of explicit theoretical specification. Given that theoretical conceptual understanding leads to operationalization for sub-sequent measurement, the unsophisticated state of affairs is reflected in the fact that most sociologists measured religiosity by simply inquiring as to frequency of church attendance or belief in God.

Beginning in the 1960's, the concept of religiosity received new theoretical attention which lead, in turn, to new and important developments in measurement. Most influential in this new treatment of the religiosity variable was the notion of multidimensional religious commitment developed by Charles Y. Glock and his associates at the University of California. Glock's article "On the Study of Religious Commitment" (1962) set in motion a series of renewed theoretical and empirical efforts that have continued for the past 18 years. These developments are discussed in Part One of this book.

This book is a compilation of some of the efforts inspired by Glock's work. Contained in this volume are some of the Author's research and conceptual thinking on religiosity over a period of 13 years. The works presented herein can serve to provide students and colleagues with valuable insights into the general flavor of recent works of sociologists of religion on the important variable of religiosity.

Jerry D. Cardwell
Longwood College
Farmville, Virginia

ix

Photograph by James G. Silliman, Jr.
Longwood College

"Nothing that exists is an island unto itself;...
everything that holds membership in the world is
an element of a seamless garment - the 'ragged
edges' of every individual reality splay off into
those of another, and the world is a wedding."

Nathan Scott

PART ONE

MODERN DEVELOPMENTS IN RELIGIOSITY

THE THEORY OF MULTIDIMENSIONAL RELIGIOSITY: CONCEPTUAL, THEORETICAL, AND EMPIRICAL DEVELOPMENTS

Jerry D. Cardwell

Religiosity is a widely used but difficult concept to define and consequently has traditionally been a difficult concept for sociologists to research. In the not too distant past, one or two factors such as church attendance or belief in God have been used as item indicants of the more inclusive concept of religiosity. Recently, due in large part to the pioneering work of Charles Y. Glock and his associates, religiosity has been subdivided into various dimensions. Today, most sociologists would agree that the use of a single criterion to provide an accurate reflection of the concept of religiosity covers too broad an area to be considered meaningful. This paper traces the development of the multidimensional conceptualization of religiosity, assesses its present state of development, suggests some current problems, and explores possible prospects for the future.

All professional sociologists recognize that their discipline is affected in no small measure by the continuing processes of empirical research, conceptual development,

1

and theoretical breakthrough, and that often the results of these events have the impact of reordering or reshaping the discipline in the fashion suggested by Thomas S. Kuhn's analysis of the structure of scientific revolutions. We believe that Glock's work has had such an impact on the sociology of religion. Although the words "reordering" or "reshaping" might be too strong to characterize the impact of Glock's work, it is clearly safe to say that it has served to revitalize interest in the sociology of religion. To be frank, we believe the theoretical-conceptual-empirical interest and research generated by Glock's formulations are a result of one of the two major intellectual events in the sociology of religion in the past twenty-five years. (The other major intellectual event is Bellah's notion of Civil Religion). It is surprising, therefore, that a major effort has not been made to tie the events surrounding these developments together for students and colleagues in sociology.

Precise identification of the beginning of theoretical breakthrough is not an easy task. Human thought, whether philosophical, scientific, or theological, is generally a cumulative process in which the parameters of significant theoretical ephocs are not always clearly defined. What often gives the impression of being a clearly defined theoretical breakthrough capable of dealing with long-standing anomalies can usually be easily tied to earlier arguments I call "anticipatory arguments." An anticipatory argument can best be understood as falling into that category of disquieting works that point to the perceived inadequacies in a given theoretical-conceptual-empirical domain of inquiry. Thus, anticipatory arguments have the character of pointing out conceptual difficulties and suggesting possible avenues of resolution, but they usually stop short of providing closure for the deficiencies they illustrate. The theoretical breakthrough collects, categorizes, and collates the anomalies detected and any solutions proposed in the anticipatory arguments and generates the celebrated breakthrough. This is true of Glock's (1962) formal statement of the components and characteristics of a multi-dimensional religiosity. Thus, proper recognition should be given to those scholars who presented arguments which suggested the outlines of the foundation upon which Glock's work would ultimately be built.

It would be accurate to state that religion has commanded the attention of sociologists since the beginning of the discipline; religion has been central to much theoretical thinking in sociology for many years. As Faulkner and DeJong (1966) and others have pointed out, early thinkers such as E. B. Tylor and J. G. Frazer expressed an interest in man as a believer in transcendental beings. William James (1936) categorized religion into the dimensions of "feelings, acts, and experiences." Until recently, however, religious commitment has not been an issue of theoretical and practical interest to the sociologist of religion. Indeed, contemporary concern with developing a theoretical scheme to systematically and comprehensively assess religious commitment is most accurately traced to Charles Y. Glock's important essay written in 1962--less than twenty years ago.

Although Glock is rightfully credited with developing the initial formalized theory of multidimensional religious commitment, several sociologists of religion argued for the demise of extant modes of thinking by expressing dissatisfaction with existing, one-dimensional conceptions of religiosity and, in some instances, suggesting possible new conceptual schemes. The works of Herberg (1955), Lenski (1961), Allport (1960), and Vernon (1962) come immediately to mind and can be cited as among the contributions of the more widely known in the field of the sociology of religion. Vernon, for example, clearly anticipated a multidimensional theory of religiosity in his suggestion that:

> Such criteria as church membership, church attendance, or acceptance of specific beliefs are often considered to measure religiosity....there would seem to be a valid distinction between 'being religious' and being a church member, 'attending church,' or accepting a specific belief.

Vernon's remarks are typical of the sort also being made by Herberg and Lenski. While the aforementioned sociologists were publishing their anticipatory arguments, some parallel developments were taking shape in the psychology of religion. Most representative of the developments in psychology are the works of Allport (1960). Allport set forth two important dimensions of religious commitment, labeling them the "extrinsic" and "intrinsic" dimensions, respectively. Allport (1960:257) conceptualized his dimensions as follows:

> Extrinsic religion is a self-serving utilitarian,

3

self-protective form of religious outlook, which
provides the believer with comfort and salvation
at the expense of out-groups. <u>Intrinsic</u> religion
marks the life that has interiorized the total
creed of his faith without reservation, including
the commandment to love one's neighbor. A person
of this sort is more intent on serving his
religion than on making it serve him.

In other words, "...the extrinsically motivated person
<u>uses</u> his religion, whereas the intrinsically motivated <u>lives</u>
his religion (Allport, 1966:455)." The testability of
Allport's dimensions have presented difficult problems of
measurement, however, and their usefulness has therefore
remained at the level of orienting statements. Some sociologists have called for discarding one, or both of
Allport's dimensions (Hunt and King, 1971). (It should be
pointed out that Allport's conceptualizations characterize
"religiosity" as a social psychological phenomenon whose
measurement is to be pursued at the level of personal religiosity, whereas Glock's conceptualization approaches religiosity from the more traditional institutional model of
sociology. It may very well turn out that the extrinsic vs.
intrinsic modalities at the micro-level find expression in
a similar fashion at the macro-level. It would probably be
a worthwhile venture to begin the process of decomposition
of the macro-level dimensions outlined by Glock to specify
their content in terms of Allport's extrinsic and intrinsic
dimensions).

The primary point to be made at this juncture is that
Glock's theory of multidimensional religiosity represents
the culmination of the thoughts and contributions of many
sociologists and psychologists. While this paper will take
1962 as its starting point, much academic and scholarly work
preceded the contemporary theory of religiosity whose modern
development is to be traced and assessed.

PROPOSITIONAL STATEMENT OF GLOCK'S THEORY OF RELIGIOSITY

It is seldom that a sociological theory is stated in a
propositional form which conforms to the canons of logical
deduction. As Blalock (1970) has properly indicated,
sociological theories are usually set forth in sentences
utilizing the everyday English language. Therefore, when
introduced, they are typically presented in the ongoing

discussion of the domain of concern. A result of this state of affairs is that theoretical propositions must be abstracted from the general discussion in which they appear. Glock's theory of multidimensional religiosity is not different in this regard. Five general propositions which establish the boundaries of the theory and are given in the text of Glock's discussion can be identified. They are presented below.

P1. THE PROPOSITION OF THE UNIVERSALITY OF DIFFERENTIAL RELIGIOUS EXPECTATIONS

"Religion is not the same to all men: different religions expect quite different things of their adherents (S98)."

P2. THE PROPOSITION OF THE UNIVERSALITY OF CONSENSUS RELATIVE TO GENERAL EXPRESSION OF RELIGIOUS COMMITMENT

"There nevertheless exists among the world's religions considerable consensus as to the more general areas in which religiosity ought to be manifested (S98)."

P3. THE PROPOSITION OF GENERAL CORE DIMENSIONS OF RELIGIOSITY

"These general areas may be thought of as the core dimensions of religiosity (S98)."

P4. THE PROPOSITION OF THE UNIVERSALITY OF THE CORE DIMENSIONS OF RELIGIOUS COMMITMENT

"Five core dimensions can be distinguished-- within one or another of the dimensions all of the many and diverse manifestations of religiosity can be ordered. The dimensions are identified as the experiential, ritualistic, ideological, intellectual and consequential (S98)."

P5. THE PROPOSITION OF THE GENERALITY OF THE THEORY OF RELIGIOUS COMMITMENT

"These dimensions provide a theoretical frame of reference for studying religion and assessing religiosity (S99)."

RELIGIOSITY IN 5-D: ON SUBSTANTIVE AND PROCEDURAL CLARITY

As previously stated, most sociologists of religion are in general agreement that Glock should be acknowledged as having developed the initial formalized theory of multi-dimensional religiosity. While there can be little doubt as to the importance of Glock's contribution, it is probably true that Fukuyama's (1960) research was an important factor in Glock's development of the theory. Fukuyama's research reported the results of an analysis of 4,095 questionnaires administered to members of 12 Congregational Christian Churches.[1] The churches were located in seven cities in the northwest and north-central United States. What is of primary importance for now, however, is the fact that Fukuyama provided the earliest test of the dimensions of religiosity previously outlined by Glock ("The Religious Revival in America?", in Zahn, ed., Religion and the Face of America). It must be pointed out that at this point in the development of the theory of multidimensional religiosity-- the year 1959--Glock's developing theory contained only four dimensions and had not become formalized to the point achieved in his 1962 contribution.

Fukuyama examined four dimensions of religious commitment: the cognitive, cultic, creedal, and devotional. The cognitive dimension is concerned with what individuals know about religion, i.e., religious knowledge. The cultic dimension makes reference to the individual's religious practices, i.e., ritualistic behavior. The creedal dimension is concerned with a personal religious belief, and the devotional dimension refers to a person's religious feelings and experiences, i.e., the experiential dimension.

Using a Likert type summated scale, Fukuyama classified persons as "low," "moderate," or "high" on the four dimensions. Utilizing this general scheme, he found the following for this sample of Congregationalists. First, women are more religious on the average than men on the cultic, creedal, and devotional dimensions. Men score higher than women on the cognitive dimension. In other words, Fukuyama found that men are more likely than women to "know" their religion, but less likely to practice it, believe it, and experience it. Women differ most from men on the devotional dimension. Second, there is little difference on the cognitive dimension as regards age. Third, the more highly

6

educated and the more well-to-do parishioners score higher than less educated and poorer parishioners on both the cognitive and cultic dimensions. The less educated and poorer parishioners score higher on the creedal and devotional dimensions. Finally, the cognitively oriented show the greatest resistance to having religion taught in the public schools. Resistance decreases in this order: cognitive, cultic, creedal, and devotional. Fukuyama also found that the cognitively oriented are most likely to grant their ministers the right to preach on controversial subjects and to favor a racially inclusive membership.

In general, Fukuyama's work reported on research that presented early confirmation of Glock's preliminary thinking on the multidimensional theory of religiosity. It is probably Fukuyama's confirmation of Glock's early thinking that led him to devote his attention to formalizing his theory of multidimensional religiosity which appeared somewhat later in his 1962 article.[2]

As he indicated in his general statement of the theory, Glock did not maintain that a measure of high religiosity on any one criteria necessarily implied a corresponding measure on any other criteria. It is possible, as Glock points out, that one measure of religiosity may be negatively correlated with another, or a second measure of religiosity. Thus, a religious response on one dimension of religiosity is not a priori necessary for attributing a religious response on any other dimension of religiosity[3]. Presumably, however, each of the dimensions of religious commitment is a subset of a larger configuration. Furthermore, one cannot escape the impression that the five dimensions taken collectively are the larger configuration identified as religious commitment. It seems reasonable, therefore, that the "epistemic" correlation between dimensions would be positive.

In terms of developing the theory of religiosity, we believe Glock's (1962) statement provided a clear analysis of the substantive content of the dimensions of religiosity. Procedural clarity, therefore, was the next logical step in the full development of the theory. If it is granted that Glock provided clear substantive categories, it nevertheless remained problematic as to the adequacy of the measures the categories would yield. Stated in a different manner, research was needed to address the question of the scalability of the dimensions of religious commitment. The problem of scalability is not trivial precisely because substantive theoretical categories are not particularly useful in social science if valid measures thereof cannot be developed. Without valid measures of at least certain segments of the theory the possibility of refutation is not acknowledged, and the theory is thus not admissible into scientific discourse. Therefore, the question of whether the substantive definitions would yield parallel procedural (operational) definitions which would, in turn, prove to be scalable remained a paramount question. Faulkner and DeJong (1966) addressed this important aspect of the theory of religiosity.

According to Faulkner and DeJong, the problem which they addressed was "to develop measures of religiosity for each of the five dimensions using the Guttman scale technique." Their research was based on "the framework suggested by Glock (1966:247)." Their sample was composed of 362 members of sociology classes at the Pennsylvania State University.

Twenty-three procedural definitions which were believed to parallel Glock's substantive definitions were chosen as item indicants of the five dimensions. Dichotomized responses on each item, within dimensions, were analyzed for scalability. The items were acceptable on both logical and empirical grounds. The ideological dimension yielded a coefficient of reproducibility of .94 and asked such questions as belief relative to the end of the world, and the nature of the Deity. The intellectual scale yielded a coefficient of .93 and was composed of items which measured how well an individual was informed about basic tenets and cotrine of his religious faith. Ritualism produced a coefficient of reproducibility of .92 and asked traditional ritualism questions such as church attendance and frequency of prayer. The experiential dimension coefficient of reproducibility was .92, while the consequential dimension was .90. Scalable items were easiest to obtain for the ideological dimension on the one hand, and most difficult for the consequential dimension on the other hand.

As Faulkner and DeJong (1966:252) state, their research was conducted in order to "empirically test the interrelationships among scales for five dimensions of religiosity as identified by Glock (1962)." Using Guttman scaling criteria, all scales were found to be substantially above the minimum level of acceptability for scalability. Therefore, Faulkner and DeJong state that the connection between

8

substantive and procedural definitions, while remaining epistemic in nature, suggest an acceptable logical connection between the theoretical and research levels.

Weigert and Thomas (1969), however, seriously question the connection between substantive and procedural definitions established by Faulkner and DeJong (1966). They criticize the "equivocation which may result from violation of natural language or face validity . . . ." and maintain that the research of Faulkner and DeJong presents an excellent example of this equivocation (1969:260). To the extent that Weigert and Thomas cast doubt on the connection between substantive and procedural definitions developed by Faulkner and DeJong, they also cast doubt upon the specification of the substantive content of Glock's theory and, therefore, offer partial refutation of it. In our opinion, however, the argument of Weigert and Thomas is at best incorrect, and at worse shows somewhat of a misunderstanding of the nature and role of sociological theory. Weigert and Thomas (1969:260) are concerned with "the gap between stimulus and concept." Their major complaint against Faulkner and DeJong is stated as:

> Qua sociologist, the relevant explanation for the acceptance or rejection of a posited link between the concept and a measured event, i.e., the event as known, is the prevailing norms and expectations of the scientific community concerning the nature of evidence and the form of inference. In the Faulkner and DeJong article, these expectations are violated (1969:260).

It is clear that Weigert and Thomas are making an appeal to what Feyerabend has called the consistency condition to serve as a basis for their critical remarks. (For a discussion of the consistency condition in sociological theory, see Cardwell (1979)). The consistency condition states that only such rules for observation are admissible in a given domain. Now, in making their appeal to the consistency condition, Weigert and Thomas are indeed intolerant. As previously stated, if taken seriously, their argument represents a partial refutation of the theory. But their argument would not eliminate the theory because the theory is in disagreement with the facts. Rather, their argument would eliminate the theory because it is in disagreement with another system of evidence and form of inference; with a system of evidence and form of inference, moreover, whose confirming instances it may share. Such criticism does not make an a priori case against the connection between substantive and procedural definition which has been established by Faulkner and DeJong (1966).

Although the applicability of the theory of religious commitment to acceptable procedural operations was given support by Faulkner and DeJong, the question of the breadth of the composite concept of religiosity was as yet unanswered. Essentially, the number of dimensions of religiosity now became a salient question.

Morton King (1967) provided the initial investigation into the possibility of religious commitment having a content of more than five dimensions. Using a factor analytic technique (principle axis solution), King sampled 575 active and inactive members of six Methodist congregations in the City of Dallas, Texas, and its suburbs. The sample was selected by purposive sampling methods in order to provide a wide range of subjects different in socio-economic status, mean age of congregation represented, age composition of individual members, and congregational emphasis on matters of religion.[3]

Suspecting that religiosity was in fact composed of more than five dimensions, King's null hypothesis was that "religion is unidimensional." (H_0: Religiosity is composed of only one dimension.) King reports two related findings: (1) the hypothesis of the unidimensionality of religious commitment must be rejected for these data, and the multidimensional view of religiosity is given tentative support; and (2) nine dimensions can be identified from the items and for the subjects.[4] The nine dimensions King identified are: (1) Creedal assent and personal commitment; (2) Participation in congregational activities; (3) Personal religious experience; (4) Personal ties to the congregation; (5) Commitment to intellectual search despite doubt; (6) Openness to religious growth; (7) Dogmatism; (8) Extrinsic orientation; (8a) Financial behavior; (8b) Financial attitude; and (9) Talking and reading about religion.

What is interesting to note about King's (1967) research is that three of the nine dimensions he identified are similar to those proposed by Glock and later scaled by Faulkner and DeJong. Specifically, reference is made to the creedal assent and personal commitment; the participation in congregational activities; and the personal religious experience. These dimensions correspond to Glock's

10

ideological, ritualistic, and experiential dimensions, respectively.

As attempts to obtain substantive and procedural clarity for the theory gained momentum, Richard Clayton (1968) replicated Faulkner and DeJong's (1966) study of Pennsylvania State University students using students from Stetson University, a small, private, liberal arts university in the South. According to Clayton (1968:80), "Using Glock's conceptual framework as a model, Faulkner and DeJong constructed five Guttman-type religiosity scales which seem to be both methodologically and statistically sound." Clayton arrived at two major conclusions based on his study (Clayton 1968:83):

> First, the Religiosity in 5-D Scale seems to be a valuable methodological contribution to the sociology of religion. Second, the propensity for religiosity seems to be higher for students at a small, private, church-related university in the South than for students at a large state university in the Northeast.

Thus, Clayton's work provided additional evidence that the hypotheses generated by Glock's theory were acceptable on both substantive and procedural grounds and this additional research helped pave the way for the studies on predictive clarity that were to follow.

Interestingly, along with Cardwell (1971), Verbit (1970), Finner (1971) and Klemmack and Cardwell (1973), Clayton, working alone (1971) and with James W. Gladden (1974), would later come to question the theory of religiosity and, by implication, his own work. Of course, such developments are in fact expected and crucial to the full development of any theory.

Upon re-examination of King's (1967) original data, King and Hunt (1969) presented some amended findings. Their amended findings dropped some items from dimensions, added others, and shifted others. Additionally, they expanded the number of dimensions they could isolate from nine to eleven. The hypothesis of multidimensionality, however, remained intact.

In general, there is ample evidence (Fukuyama, 1960; Faulkner and DeJong, 1966; King, 1967; Clayton, 1968; and

11

King and Hunt, 1969) to suggest that the substantive definitions set forth by Glock were sufficiently enumerated to provide acceptable parallel procedural (operational) definitions. This is to be expected if the notion of construct validity is not violated, i.e., if there is an essential correspondence between substantive and procedural elements. It is a credit to Glock that he was acutely aware of this requirement. In addition to considering substantive problems, Glock also considered the "questioning of what is required for a comprehensive and operationally useful definition of religiousness, and (suggested) a research strategy for meeting these requirements." That Faulkner and DeJong, King, Clayton, and King and Hunt were able to achieve empirical results based on the substantive categories demonstrates Glock's success.

Once having moved from substantive to procedural clarity, the next step in the full testing of the theory must address the question of the predictive ability of the several dimensions of religiosity. The question that now presented itself was whether the knowledge of the score on the "X" variable (the multidimensional measure of religious commitment) contributes significantly[5] to the ability to predict the score on a "Y", or dependent, variable. Several possible configurations of religious commitment as a predictor are apparent, at least pragmatically. First, it is possible that ritualistic behavior or some other sub-scale of religious commitment is the best possible predictor, and that knowledge of the scores on the remaining sub-scales does not contribute significantly to the ability to predict. Second, it could be that each of the five sub-scales add equal amounts to the ability to predict. If so, all five sub-scales should be taken into account when making predictive statements based on a knowledge of a religious commitment score. Third, it is possible that two or three, or some other combination of the sub-scales allow prediction with a high degree of proficiency, and that the inclusion of the remaining sub-scales does not add appreciably to the ability to predict. The question then becomes as follows: If we desire to predict a variable "Y" from knowledge of religious commitment (the "X" or independent variable), which sub-scales of religious commitment should be utilized in making the predictive statement. In moving from procedural to predictive clarity, these and other fundamental questions must be addressed and successfully answered.

THE THEORY OF RELIGIOUS COMMITMENT: FROM PROCEDURAL TO PREDICTIVE CLARITY

In attempting to move from procedural to predictive clarity, the essential question to be asked is the extent to which religious commitment contributes to an understanding of some selected dependent variable. Cardwell (1969) provided the initial research concerning the predictive utility of a multidimensional measure of religious commitment. He reasoned that the test of the predictive ability should center on a dependent variable whose relation to unidimensional measures of religious commitment had previously been demonstrated.[6] If Glock's (1962) theory was an improvement over previous theoretical efforts, the resulting data should provide new insights into the relation of religious commitment to the dependent variable.[7] Attitudes toward premarital sexual permissiveness was chosen as the dependent variable out of deference to the large number of previous studies indicating an inverse relationship between it and unidimensional religious commitment.

Using a sample of 187 New England college students, five dimensions of religious commitment were measured by the Likert technique and tested for significance of relationship to attitudes toward premarital sexual permissiveness. It was hypothesized that the composite measure of religious commitment and each of the five sub-scales of religious commitment would be inversely related to attitudes toward premarital sexual permissiveness.

As regards the question of whether the religious variable is composed of more than one dimension, the answer according to this research, is yes. It was ascertained that each of the five sub-scales of religious commitment were highly correlated with the composite measure of religious commitment. It was safe to assume, therefore, that each sub-scale was actually measuring some dimension of the larger configuration Glock (1962) identified as religious commitment. This fact, combined with the fact that the intercorrelations among the sub-scales were substantially less than unity indicated that each sub-scale was measuring a different aspect of religious commitment. Thus, the evidence indicated that the hypothesis that religious commitment is a multidimensional concept should be given serious consideration.

To test the hypothesis that multidimensional religious commitment is a more adequate predictive variable than as it had been previously conceptualized, six hypotheses suggested an inverse relationship between (1) the multidimensional measure of religious commitment and each of the five sub-scales thereof, and (2) attitudes toward premarital sexual permissiveness. All six of these hypotheses were accepted. Each zero-order Pearsonian product moment correlation was significant at the .05 level.

What is also interesting to note, is that the correlation between religious commitment sub-scales and attitudes toward premarital sexual permissiveness suggests that frequently when researchers have used one-dimensional measures of religious commitment, they have relied on a measure that is a less accurate predictor than other sub-scale or one-dimensional measures. Historically, frequency of church attendance has been the indicator most often used as a measure of religious commitment. The data in this study confirm that ritualistic behavior is significantly related to attitudes toward premarital sexual permissiveness. The zero-order r between these two variables was -.44. However, at least two of the other sub-scales of religiosity had a higher correlation with the dependent variable. The religious knowledge sub-scale had an r of -.48, and the religious self-definition sub-scale had an r of -.49 with the dependent variable. Thus, the evidence suggests that either religious knowledge or religious self-definition would be more accurate indicators of religious commitment than ritualistic behavior. Cardwell's (1969) research suggested that Glock's (1962) theory is indeed an improvement over the predictive ability of previous unidimensional conceptions of religiosity.

Finner and Gamache (1969) also provided qualified support for the predictive ability of the multidimensional measure of religious commitment. Their dependent variable was attitudes toward induced abortion. The study tested the hypothesis that a multidimensional measure of religious commitment is directly related to attitudes toward induced abortion. The data used by Finner and Gamache came from 122 mailed questionnaires given to a stratified random sample of residents of a small (population 4,000) northern New England community. These researchers found that the composite commitment scale was related to attitudes toward induced abortion at the .04 level. Finner and Gamache concluded, therefore, that qualified support could be given to the hypothesis of a positive relationship between religiosity as measured using a multidimensional scale and attitudes toward induced

14

abortion.

Ruppel (1970) re-examined and replicated the previous research reported by Cardwell (1969). The data for Ruppel's study were acquired by means of administration of a questionnaire to a fixed place random sample of 437 freshman and senior students at Northern Illinois University during the first semester of 1966-67. The scales used to tap religiosity and premarital sexual permissiveness were identical to those used in the research reported earlier. Both scales met the .90 minimum standard for the coefficient of reproducibility. A replication of the results previously obtained should, therefore, provide greater support for the predictive ability of the concept of religiosity. Ruppel (1970:654) reports that:

> When the sub-scales which tapped the five dimensions of religiosity in this research were correlated with permissiveness, all five dimensions were significantly correlated in a negative manner with permissiveness. These findings support those recently reported by Cardwell (1969) in which the intercorrelations between religiosity and permissiveness were negative and significant, thus providing support for the multidimensional conceptual framework for religiosity.

In general, therefore, available research suggests that Glock's theory of multidimensional religious commitment does have predictive ability. Furthermore, research relating religiosity to attitudes toward premarital sexual permissiveness uncovered new relationships between religious commitment and the dependent variable, i.e., it was demonstrated that traditional measures of religiosity were not as accurate as other dimensions of the multidimensional measure. Predictive clarity has, therefore, been given at least qualified support.

THE THEORY OF RELIGIOSITY: QUESTIONS OF GENERALITY OF APPLICATION

In terms of the established criteria for what counts for acceptable substantive, procedural, and predictive clarity, Glock's (1962) theory of religious commitment appears to have received tentative support. Even in light of the several confirming studies (Cardwell, 1969; Finner and Gamache, 1969; Ruppel, 1970), however, new and important questions were being directed at the theory. Some socio-

ogists were concerned over the manner in which the ubiqui-
tousness of the theoretical framework was being taken for
granted. Specifically, researchers were asking two related
questions: (1) what evidence is there to suggest that proposition three of Glock's theory argues for developing
general core dimensions which are applicable across various
denominations; and (2) what evidence is there to indicate
that an individual who is a member of a certain religious
denomination will be religiously committed in a manner consistent with that denomination. As stated previously, it
is entirely within the realm of reason that a comprehensive
measure of religiosity cannot be achieved. It is also
reasonable to suspect that religious preference may be more
salient in terms of religious commitment than is denominational membership.

The Theory of Religiosity: Ubiquitous or Specific. A
curious series of misleading assumptions seem to have paralleled the development, operationalization, and testing of
Glock's theory of religious commitment. When researchers
have studied one-denominational group and succeeded in
devising a five-dimensional scale of religiosity which
applies thereto, they have apparently assumed that comprehensive measures of religious commitment, across denominations, have been derived. Apparently Faulkner and DeJong
(1966) did not even consider the possibility of a comprehensive measure being problematic. These researchers applied a
scale of religious commitment across the following denominations: Catholic, Jewish, Lutheran, Methodist, E.U.B.,
Presbyterian, Episcopal, and Church of Christ. In certain
instances, Faulkner and DeJong (1966:251) even combined
denominational groups. Cardwell (1971) later illustrated
that their own results suggested that they had stumbled upon
a Catholic-specific[8] scale. Other sociologists have made
similar mistaken assumptions (Cardwell, 1969; Allen and
Hites, 1961; Cline and Richards, 1965; and Finner and Gamache,
1969).

In his now famous Protestant-Catholic-Jew, Herberg (1963)
pointed out that there is probably more variation in religious expression within Protestantism than between Protestants,
Catholics and Jews. Glock and Stark (1965) asked if there is
an American Protestantism, wherein "average Protestants" can
be identified. Their conclusion is most informative for the
present discussion (1965:47):

When we speak of "protestants," therefore, we tend

16

to spin statistical fiction. It seems unjustified to consider Protestantism as a unified religious point of view in the same sense as Roman Catholicism.

Not that Roman Catholicism is monolithic either-- clearly there are several theological strands inter- woven in the Catholic church--but at least it con- stitutes an actual, organized body, Protestantism, on the other hand, includes many separate groups and the only possible grounds for treating them collectively would be if they shared a common religious vision. _This is clearly not the case_. (Italics supplied.)

Thus, evidence seems to suggest that attempts to verify Glock's (1962) theory with a comprehensive measure of multi- dimensional religious commitment cannot succeed. This is precisely because a comprehensive measure would have to assume that denominations share a common religious vision that can be tapped for the several denominations; an assump- tion, in other words, "that is clearly not the case."

Those who attempted to derive comprehensive measures of religiosity may claim, however, that the ecumenical movement suggests the correctness of their research. However, research conducted by Hadden (1967) would indicate, on the contrary, that the ecumenical movement lends support to the argument for denomination specific measures being put forth here. Hadden's data were obtained from completed question- naires returned by 7,441 parish ministers. He addressed the question of whether the differences among the various faiths were disappearing, i.e., an ecumenical movement is occurring. His conclusion (1967:64) was that there was an ecumenical movement, but that:

a major source of ecumenical unity stems from a consensus that the church has an activist responsi- bility in the world and that this mission may better be accomplished together rather than through the diversified energies of many groups. In other words, the _sources_ of _ecumenicism_ _are_ _social_ _rather_ _than_ _doctrinal_. (Italics supplied.)

The implications of Hadden's research seem clear. If a comprehensive measure can be devised, it is possible only for the consequential dimension. The remaining four dimen- sions concern doctrinal issues, which Hadden illustrates are not ingredients of an ecumenicism.

As regards another question revolving around the theory of religious commitment, Finner (1971) has completed research into the utility of both religious membership and religious preference as indicators of religiosity. Finner's study is based on questionnaires completed by 405 students at three eastern colleges. As regards this question, Finner (1971:9) concludes:

> . . .1) religious preference and religious member-
> ship are not interchangeable, 2) preference is more
> strongly related to other measures of religiosity
> than membership, and 3) using membership as the sole
> indicator of religion creates categories of people
> who vary as much within as between.

Whether or not Finner's findings would affect the use of multidimensional measures of religiosity is an empirical question. It seems reasonable, however, that a Southern Baptist who scores low on a Baptist-specific scale <u>could</u> score high on a Methodist-specific scale, if he <u>preferred</u> the latter denomination over the former. Perhaps the safest tack to take is to secure responses to questions about both membership and preference.

A question which will undoubtedly be raised is: What if we cannot develop a comprehensive measure of religious commitment--that would seem to imply that the researcher must develop a denomination-specific scale for each religious group he studies, and that would be a burdensome task. The answer to the question is readily apparent: Science strives to be accurate, but does not promise to be easy.

FOOTNOTES AND REFERENCES CITED

1. The exclusive use of Congregationalists illustrates the sampling procedures generally used and, subsequently, the problem of making a case for a single measure of universal religiosity (Glock's P4 and P5) which is discussed later in this paper.

2. See Glock (1962), Footnote Two, S109.

3. Nor, for that matter, is a high score on any one dimension sufficient for attributing a high score on any other dimension.

3. Here again, the sample utilized is concerned with a single religious denomination. The generalizability of these findings across religions remains, therefore, problematic.

4. Strictly speaking, factor analysis is not an hypothesis testing procedure.

5. Significantly is not intended to imply significant in any statistical sense in this statement.

6. This procedure follows the suggestion of Lazarsfeld (1966) that the criterion variable be one of which the relation to the predictor variable has been previously demonstrated.

7. "Improvement" is not used in any value definition sense.

8. Faulkner and DeJong's data are merely that--suggestive. Their data supplies the hypothesis; it does not give reason for its acceptance or rejection.

Allen, E. E. and Hites, R. W.
   1961 "Factors in Religious Attitudes of Older Adolescents." Journal of Social Psychology, 55:265-273.

Allport, G. W.
   1950 The Individual and His Religion. New York: Macmillan.

Blalock, H. M.
   1970 Theory Construction: From Verbal to Mathematical Formulations. Englewood Cliffs, New Jersey: Prentice-Hall Inc.

Cardwell, J. D.
   1969 "The Relationship Between Religious Commitment and Attitudes Toward Premarital Sexual Permissiveness: A 5-D Analysis." Sociological Analysis, 30 (Summer): 72-80

Cardwell, J. D.
   1971 "Multidimensional Measures of Interfaith Commitment: A Research Note." Pacific Sociological Review, 14 (January): 79-88

Cline, V. B. and Richards, J. M., Jr.
  1965 "A Factor-Analytic Study of Religious Belief and
        Behavior." Journal of Personality and Social
        Psychology, 1:569-578

Faulkner, J. E. and DeJong, G. F.
  1966 "Religiosity in 5-D: An Empirical Analysis."
        Social Forces, 45 (December): 246-254.

Finner, S. L. and Gamache, J. D.
  1969 "The Relation Between Religious Commitment and
        Attitudes Toward Induced Abortion." Sociological
        Analysis, 30 (Spring): 1-12.

Finner, S. L.
  1971 "Religious Membership and Religious Preference:
        Equal Indicators of Religiosity?" Journal for the
        Scientific Study of Religion, (Winter), 76-94.

Fukuyama, Yoshio
  1960 "The Major Dimensions of Church Membership." Review
        of Religious Research, 2:154-161.

Glock, Charles Y.
  1962 "On The Study of Religious Commitment." Religious
        Education (Research Supplement), 42 (July/August):
        S98-S110.

Glock, Charles Y. and Stark, Rodney
  1965 Religion and Society in Tension. Chicago, Ill:
        Rand-McNally.

Hadden, J. K.
  1967 "A Protestant Paradox--Divided They Merge."
        Trans-action, 4 (July/August): 63-69.

Herberg, W.
  1955 Protestant-Catholic-Jew. Garden City: Doubleday
        and Co.

King, Morton
  1967 "Measuring the Religious Varble: Nine Proposed
        Dimensions." Journal for the Scientific Study of
        Religion, 6: 173-190.

Lenski, Gerhard
  1963 The Religious Factor. Garden City: Doubleday and Co.

Merton, Robert K.
   1968   <u>Social Theory and Social Structure</u>.   Glencoe, Ill:
          The Free Press, (Rev. Ed.).

Ruppel, Howard J.
   1970   "Religiosity and Premarital Sexual Permissiveness:
          A Response to the Reiss-Heltsley and Broderick
          Debate."   <u>Journal of Marriage and the Family</u>,
          647-655.

Vernon, Glenn M.
   1962   <u>The Sociology of Religion</u>.   New York: McGraw-Hill
          Book Co.

PART TWO

THE MEASUREMENT OF RELIGIOSITY

THE RELATIONSHIP BETWEEN RELIGIOUS COMMITMENT AND PREMARITAL
SEXUAL PERMISSIVENESS: A FIVE DIMENSIONAL ANALYSIS*

Jerry D. Cardwell

   While there is a considerable volume of literature on the
relationship of premarital sexual permissiveness to religious
commitment, the majority is seen as unsatisfactory in terms
of tapping the religious commitment dimension (Dedman, 1959).
Most studies to date have used church attendance or church
affiliation as an indicator of religious commitment (Dedman,
1959; Wallin and Clark, 1964). Some have left the religious
factor implied in their research. Only a small portion of
previous research has, however, attempted to measure religious commitment in a more comprehensive manner (Glock, 1964).

   There has been almost continuous discussion between sociologists of religion as to what comprises an adequate measure
of religious commitment (Vernon, 1961: chapter 13). Historically, religious commitment has meant whatever it means to
"be religious." Today, however, most sociologists of religion agree that the use of a single criterion to provide a
measure of religious commitment covers too broad an area to
be scientifically accurate. Vernon (1962) has stated:

      Such criteria as church membership, church attendance
      or acceptance of specific beliefs are often considered
      to measure religiosity . . .   There would seem to be

a valid distinction between "being religious" and
being a church member, "attending church," or
accepting a specific belief.

As Charles Glock (1964) had indicated, a measure of high
religious commitment on any one criterion does not necessarily
imply a corresponding measure on any other criteria. (It is
possible, as Glock points out, that one measure of religious
commitment may be negatively correlated with a second measure
of religious commitment). Thus, a high score on any one di-
memsion of religious commitment is not a priori necessary for
attrbuting a high score on any other dimension of religious
commitment. It is reasoned, therefore, that a measure which
more adequately taps the various dimensions in which religious
commitment could be manifested should be utilized before any
scientific statements concerning the significance of the relationship between religious commitment and premarital sexual
permissiveness are made. The use of a more comprehensive
measure of religious commitment and the identification of the
relationship between religious commitment and attitudes toward
premarital sexual behavior is the central purpose of this
study.

Sociologists have not ignored the relationship between
these two social variables. Several studies have directed
their attention to this area of inquiry. The Kinsey (1953)
studies are often regarded as the most monumental contribution
to the study of human sexual behavior. In an often quoted
passage Kinsey has stated:

> The accumulative and active incidences of premarital
> coitus has been distinctly higher among those females
> in the sample who were less actively connected with
> religious groups, and lower among those who were most
> devout. This, in general, was true for Protestant,
> Catholic, and Jewish groups. There appear to be no
> other factors which affect the female's pattern of
> premarital behavior as markedly as the decade in
> which she was born and her religious background.

Following Kinsey's pioneering work, sociologists have, in
general, demonstrated that a relationship of significant magnitude exists between religious commitment and premarital
sexual activity. Studies by Lindenfeld (1960), Dedman (1959),
and Hohman and Schaffner (1947), are examples of the kind of
research which has typically been undertaken in this area.

24

THE MULTIDIMENSIONAL MEASURE OF RELIGIOUS COMMITMENT

The majority of investigations which have attempted to relate religious commitment to some other variable have used single criteria for their measure of religious commitment. Following Chalres Y. Glock (1964), this study will consider religious commitment to be composed of at least five dimensions. These dimensions will be defined as (1) the ritualistic behavior dimension, where the concern is centered on what people "do" rather than what they "think" or "believe:" (2) the religious knowledge dimension, which has to do with how well informed and knowledgeable a person is about the basic tenets of his religious faith; (3) the religious belief dimension, which measures what the respondent believes about supernatural phenomena; (4) the religious self definition dimension, which is focused on what the respondent "feels" or how he defines himself relative to his religious beliefs; and (5) the religious effects dimension, which measures the impact, or "effects" of the prior four dimensions on the everyday secular life.

Analysis of the Data

The data utilized in this study were collected from an availability sample of 187 college students in a New England State University. Due to the methodological shortcoming of the college population as a sample source, no attempt was made to assure representativeness or randomness of the population under study. The questionnaire was a Likert type summated scale which included a 30-item scale of religious commitment and a 24-item scale of attitudes toward premarital sexual permissiveness (Reiss, 1964). Multiple and partial regression equations were used in the statistical analysis of the data.

A central point of this study is the premise that a more comprehensive measure would permit a more detailed and more meaningful analysis of commitment per se, and of its relationship to other social variables. Accordingly, five dimensions of religious commitment were derived and subjected to testing. The question that now presents itself is whether the knowledge of the score on the "X" variable (the multidimensional measure of religious commitment) contributes significantly to the ability to predict the score on a "Y" variable (attitudes toward premarital sexual permissivness). Several possible configurations of religious commitment as a predictor are apparent, at least pragmatically. First, it is possible that ritualistic behavior or some other sub-scale of religious commitment is the best possible predictor (Blalock, 1966), and that knowledge of the scores on the remaining sub-scales does not contribute significantly to the ability to predict. Second, it could be that each of the five sub-scales add equal amounts to the ability to predict. If so, all five sub-scales should be taken into account when making predictive statements based on a knowledge of a religious commitment score. Third, it is possible that two or three, or some other combination of the sub-scales allow prediction with a high degree of proficiency, and that the inclusion of the remaining sub-scales does not add appreciably to the ability to predict. The question then becomes as follows: If we desire to predict a variable "Y" from knowledge of religious commitment (the "X" variable), which sub-scales of religious commitment should be utilized in making the predictive statement?

Use of the computational procedure for multiple correlation provides information concerning the contribution of each sub-scale of religious commitment to the composite scale of religious commitment, i.e., the proportion of variation in the composite religious commitment scale that can be explained by each of the five sub-scales of religious commitment. Here we have defined the five sub-scales of religious commitment as independent variables and the composite scale as the dependent variable. However, each sub-scale variable is part of the composite scale of religious commitment, and when taken together they are the composite scale. Therefore, we are, in effect, correlating a variable with itself. Such a procedure aids us, however, in understanding the manner in which each sub-scale measure contributes to the composite measure of religious commitment. Table One provides information as to the proportion of variation in religious commitment explained by the five sub-scales of religious commitment.

We can now state the hypotheses tested with these data. Our first hypothesis concerns the relationship of the composite measure of religious commitment to attitudes toward premarital sexual permissiveness, and is stated as follows:

Hypothesis 1. There is an inverse relationship between religious commitment and permissive attitudes toward premarital sex, i.e., the higher the religious commitment the less permissive will be the attitudes toward premarital sex.
Hypothesis 2. There is an inverse relationship between

each of the five sub-scales of religious commitment and permissive attitudes toward premarital sex, i.e., the higher the religious commitment on each sub-scale the less permissive will be the attitudes toward premarital sex.

Hypothesis Two, stated above, concerns the relationship of each of the five sub-scales of religious commitment to attitudes toward premarital sexual permissiveness.

TABLE 1
Proportion of Variation in
Religious Commitment Explained by
the Five Sub-Scales of
Religious Commitment
(r^2 Value)

Religious Commitment Sub-Scale	Proportion of Variation Explained
Religious Belief	.82*
Ritualistic Behavior	.91*
Religious Knowledge	.96*
Religious Effects	.99**
Religious Self-Definitions	---

*Significant at the .05 level
**Did not enter into the regression equation

In considering Hypothesis One, we are concerned with the composite measure of religious commitment and its relationship to attitudes toward premarital sexual permissiveness. Specifically, we hypothesized that as the religious commitment score increased, the permissiveness score for the sample would decrease. We were led to hypothesize this relationship between the variables on the basis of past research in the area. As was pointed out earlier, the majority of the studies have utilized one-dimensional measures of religious commitment in their investigation. It was reasoned, therefore, that the use of a composite measure would add significant support to the previously established relationship, if such a relationship were found to obtain between the composite measure and attitudes toward premarital sexual permissiveness. The possibility existed, of course, that the one-dimensional measures were not adequate indicators of religious commitment and that the relationship established by their use was spurious. It was possible, therefore, for the correlation between the composite measure of religious commitment and sttitudes toward premarital sexual permissiveness not to be significant. Table Two presents the data used to test Hypothesis One.

The zero-order correlation between the composite measure of religious commitment and attitudes toward premarital sexual permissiveness is -.53, and is significant at the .05 level. That is, there is an inverse relationship between the two variables. Since the correlation is in the expected direction and is significant at the .05 level, the first hypothesis is accepted.

TABLE 2

Zero-Order Correlations of the Religious Commitment Scale
and Sub-Scales with Attitudes Toward Premarital
Sexual Permissiveness
(r Value)

Religious Commitment Scale	Attitudes Toward Premarital Sexual Permissiveness
Composite Scale of Religious Commitment	-.53*
Religious Effects Sub-Scale	-.40*
Ritualistic Behavior Sub-Scale	-.44*
Religious Belief Sub-Scale	-.39*
Religious Knowledge Sub-Scale	-.48*
Religious Self-Definition Sub-Scale	-.49*

*Significant at the .05 level

With Hypothesis Two, we were concerned with the single sub-scales of religious commitment. We hypothesized the same inverse relationship between the variables as with Hypothesis One. There was some doubt, however, as to whether or not the religious effects sub-scale was measuring the same phenomena as were the remaining four sub-scales. However, the zero-order correlation between the composite scale of religious commitment and the religious effects sub-scale is sufficient to confirm the accuracy of the sub-scale measuring instrument. The zero-order correlation is .65, and significant at the .05 level.

With respect to Hypothesis Two, Table Two presents the data used to test the hypothesis. Examining Table Two, we find that the zero-order correlation between attitudes toward premarital sexual permissiveness and the religious effects, ritualistic behavior, religious belief, religious knowledge, and religious self-definitions sub-scales are -.40, -.44, -.39, -.48, and -.49 respectively. Each of the correlations is significant at the .05 level. That is, the hypothesized inverse relationship between the variables is apparent. Again, as with Hypothesis One, the correlations are in the expected direction and are significant at the .05 level. Therefore, Hypothesis Two is accepted for these data.

Discussion

Religion provides man with defintions of what is moral and immoral, what is good and bad, and what is righteous and un-righteous (Vernon, 1962). According to Vernon (1965:362):

Without biologically given drives or motivators to
guide his interaction, man develops symbolic guides
which he follows. He acquires definitions as to what
he and others should do, and how they should relate
themselves to each other. Approved patterns he calls
good, fair, just, or moral. Disapproved patterns
carry reverse labels. Man learns the moral system
of his society and learns to want to have such a moral
system. He learns to look for and to find a moral
aspect of behavior. Once he accepts the premise that
there is, in fact, a moral dimension, he is faced with
the task of taking this dimension into account for
the various aspects of living. Religious definitions
are used by man to make moral sense out of his
experience.

Since religion provides moral definitions for man's behavior we should expect to find religious definitions regarding acceptable and unacceptable, or moral and immoral sexual behavior. We would expect, further, to find these definitions reflected, at least to some degree, in man's actual sexual behavior.

Traditionally, religion has been opposed to premarital sexual activity of any kind. As Reiss (1960) has stated, "All of our major Protestant, Catholic, and Jewish groups condemn premarital copulation." This study, as have others, has found that religious commitment does seem to affect our sexual standards and behavior. Generally, the more devout individuals are more conservative sexually.

The religious effects dimension is concerned with the responsibility aspect of religion. That is, the religion prescribes what is acceptable or unacceptable behavior in the secular world. It enumerates, as Glock and Stark (1965: 34) has made clear, the religious responsibilities of the individual. It is highly improbable that religion would be so viable in our society if it did not have consequences for the individual in the secular world. Thus, the more religious a person, the more likely it is that he will conform to those attitudes and behaviors that are consistent with his religion.

With respect to ritualistic behavior we found that as the measure of church attendance and frequency of prayer increases, attitudes toward premarital sexual activity become less permissive. This finding is consistent with almost all previous studies into this area. Various studies have found that there is a wide discrepancy between the reporting of a belief in God, and attendance at a church (Glock and Stark, 1965: 68-85). However, we have found a high correlation between ritualistic behavior and religious belief (.74). This finding seems to be in general agreement with the findings of Ferking (1965), who found that cultic and devotional participation before coming to college were highly significant in relation to all levels of participation. These data seem to reaffirm the contention that many of the basic patterns of religious participation are established before the students come to campus. The college environment may serve to reinforce and/or accentuate the prevailing patterns of religious participation for students.

The research reported herein found that generally the stronger a person's religious belief, the less permissive will be his attitudes toward premarital sex. The items included in the questionnaire to measure religious belief were designed to serve as indicators of belief in terms of traditional church doctrine, and, therefore, what Glock and Stark (1965: 24) have termed the "belief structure" of religion. While we did find that strong religious belief was correlated to permissiveness, its correlation was lower than any of the other four sub-scales of religious commitment. One possible reason for this dimension having the lowest correlation is that it provides information concerning that a person"believes," and there is often a discrepancy between what one believes and how one behaves. Of course, there is no necessary relationship between belief and related behavior. The usual interpretation of any discrepancy is that nonverbal behavior is the "true" behavior and the stated belief (if it is different) is the "untrue" behavior. It might, however, be the reverse. Individuals can "lie" verbally, but they can lie behaviorally as well. We are more concerned with establishing the relationships between both types of behavior and identifying the situational factors which help account for any differences which obtain. Therefore, the question of the salience of one's beliefs--or how important the beliefs he holds are for the individual--is of central importance. Thus, it is one thing to "believe" in traditional church doctrine, but an entirely different matter for one to be guided in his behavior by his beliefs. However, even though the correlation for this dimension was the lowest, what we have found for these data is that individuals usually do act in accordance with their religious belief, at least as regards attitudes toward premarital sexual permissiveness. Also, when taken in the context of the multidimensional measure of religious commitment, the belief dimension takes on more meaning. As Glock and Stark (1965:26) have stated:

> But the salience of belief is more appropriately studied in terms of the kind of religiosity individuals express on other dimensions. How active one is ritualistically, the kinds of religious experience he has, how well informed he is religiously, and the extent to which he acts out his beliefs in practice are all measures of the saliency of belief.

A second possible explanation of religious belief having the lowest correlation with attitudes toward premarital sexual permissiveness lies in the nature of the campus mores. As Vernon (1962:78) has made clear:

> Sociologists distinguish between norms not only on
> the basis of their content but also on the basis of
> the degree of importance a society attaches to each
> norm. . . . Those forms of behavior which a society
> feels to be imperative are called mores; those of
> lesser concern folkways. . . . Whatever the content
> of the mores of any particular group they tend to be
> reinforced by religion.

The social nature of man virtually insures that all
individuals are influenced by some value systems, and that
various subsystems both exert an influence on their beliefs
and behavior and provide a rationale to be used in following courses of thought or behavior (Bell 1966: 160). In
dealing with a college sample, we are dealing with what is
in many respects an atypical example. This atypicality may
be a reflection of the fact that premarital sexual activity
is not condemned as strongly by the individual's campus sub-
group as it is by his home community, coupled with the fact
that the student is not under the constraint of his parents
to behave in accordance with his espoused beliefs. It seems
clear, however, that one's religious beliefs have a significant effect on his attitudes toward premarital sexual permissiveness.

Our hypothesis concerning religious knowledge was supported. One fact seems to be clear in the interpretation
of this finding. All religious groups expect that the religious knowledge increases, his acceptance of traditional
religious restrictions on his behavior also increases.

In terms of religious self-definitions, we hypothesized
that there would be an inverse relationship between religious self-definitions and attitudes toward premarital
sexual permissiveness. The data clearly substantiate this
hypothesis. According to Vernon (1965: 364-365):

> Top-intensity value definitions which are defined
> as being related to a supernatural realm and/or
> beings, could not long exist in a society without
> influencing the self-definitions of the members.

Self-definitions involve the process of attributing a
definition of oneself to oneself. The fact that religion
has been such an important element in our society is sufficient to warrant the discussion of religious self-
definitions. In keeping with Vernon, it would be almost

32

impossible for an individual to long exist in our society without religion influencing his self-definitions.

Now the fact that religion does influence self-definitions allows at least two possible ways of viewing oneself relative to religion: (1) one may be convinced that his behavior is in harmony with the behavioral standards set by religion, or (2) one may define himself as at variance with religious behavioral standards. The data which was collected for this study indicates that those individuals who have strong religious self-definitions also define themselves as in harmony with the behavioral standards religion has set forth relative to premarital sexual activity. For those who define themselves as at variance with religion, we would expect to find, based on our data, increasing permissiveness as regards premarital sexual activity. For those who define themselves as religious, engaging in premarital sexual activity would involve behavior which was incompatible with their self-definitions, and feelings such as guilt or anxiety might result. The price of resolving the guilt feelings may be, too high a price to pay. For those who do not define themselves as religious, there is little reason to expect that religion would act as a restraint on their premarital sexual permissiveness. It is entirely possible, of course, for an individual not to define himself as religious but to still have restrictive attitudes toward premarital sexual behavior. The extent to which this is true is an empirical question which can only be resolved through further scientific investigation.

TABLE 3
Intercorrelation Matrix of the
Five Sub-Scales of Religious
Commitment
(r Value)

	1	2	3	4	5
1	1.00				
2	.78	1.00			
3	.54	.59	1.00		
4	.74	.81	.62	1.00	
5	.46	.52	.40	.51	1.00

Note: 1=Ritualistic Behavior
       2=Religious Self-Definitions
       3=Religious Knowledge
       4=Religious Belief
       5=Religious Effects

Summary

As regards the question of whether the religious variable is composed of more than one dimension, the answer according to this research, is yes. We found that each of the five sub-scales of religious commitment was highly correlated with the composite measure of religious commitment. It was safe to assume, therefore, that each sub-scale was actually measuring some dimension of the larger configuration we have called religious commitment. This fact, combined with the fact that the intercorrelations among the sub-scales were substantially less than unity--as shown in Table Three-- indicated that each sub-scale was measuring a different aspect of religious commitment. Thus, the evidence indicates that the hypothesis that religious commitment is a multidimensional variable should be given serious consideration.

To further test the hypothesis that religious commitment is a multidimensional variable, six hypotheses suggested an inverse relationship between (1) the multidimensional measure of religious commitment and each of the five sub-scales of religious commitment, and (2) attitudes toward premarital sexual permissiveness. All six of these hypotheses were accepted. Each correlation was significant at the .05 level.

Thus, the data seems to indicate quite clearly that religious commitment is a multidimensional phenomenon, and that when used in the context of social research, all five of the sub-scales should be taken into account.

What is also interesting to note, is that the correlation between the religious commitment sub-scales and attitudes toward premarital sexual permissiveness suggests that frequently when researchers have used one-dimensional measures of religious commitment, they have relied on a measure that is a less accurate predictor than other sub-scale, or one-dimensional measures. Historically, frequency of church attendance has been the indicator most often used as a measure of religious commitment. The data in this study confirm that ritualistic behavior is significantly related to attitudes toward premarital sexual permissiveness. The zero-order correlation between these two variables is -.44. However, at least two of the other sub-scales of religious commitment have a higher correlation with attitudes toward premarital sexual permissiveness. The religious knowledge sub-scale has a correlation of -.48 with attitudes toward premarital sexual permissiveness, and the religious self-definitions sub-scale has a correlation of -.49 with permissiveness. Thus, the evidence suggests that either religious knowledge or religious self-definitions would be more accurate indicators of religious commitment than ritualistic behavior.

FOOTNOTES AND REFERENCES CITED

* Reprinted from Sociological Analysis, Vol. 30, No. 2, Summer, 1969, with permission.

Bell, Robert R.
  1966 Premarital Sex in a Changing Society. Englewood Cliffs, N.J.: Prentice-Hall.

Blalock, Hubert M.
  1966 Social Statistics. New York: McGraw-Hill.

Dedman, Jean.
  1959 "The Relationship Between Religious Attitude and Attitude Toward Premarital Sex Relations." Marriage and Family Living 21 (May): 171-176.

Ferking, Ken.
  1965 "Religious Participation of Lutheran Students." Review of Religious Research 6 (Winter): 153-162.

Glock, Charles Y.
  1962 "On the Study of Religious Commitment." Religious Education (Research Supplement) 42 (July-August): s98-s110.

Glock, Charles Y., and Rodney Stark.
  1965 Religion and Society in Tension. Chicago: Rand-McNally.

Hohman, Leslie B., and Bertram Schaffner.
  1947 "The Sex Lives of Unmarried Men." American Journal of Sociology 52 (May): 501-507.

Kinsey, Alfred C., et al.
  1953 Sexual Behavior in the Human Female. Philadelphia: W. B. Saunders.

Lindenfeld, Frank.
1960 "A Note on Social Mobility, Religiosity, and Students' Attitudes Toward Premarital Sexual Relations." American Sociological Review 25 (February) 81-84.

Reiss, Ira L.
1960 Premarital Sexual Standards in America. Glencoe: Free Press.

1964 "The Scaling of Premarital Sexual Permissiveness." Marriage and Family Living 26 (May): 188-198.

Vernon, Glenn M.
1962 The Sociology of Religion. New York: McGraw-Hill.

1965 Human Interaction: An Introduction to Sociology. New York: Ronald.

Wallin, Paul, and Alexander L. Clark
1964 "Religiosity, Sexual Gratification and Marital Satisfaction in the Middle Years of Life." Social Forces 42 (March): 303-309.

MULTIDIMENSIONAL MEASURES OF INTERFAITH COMMITMENT: A RESEARCH NOTE*

Jerry D. Cardwell

Historically, sociologists of religion have defined religious commitment as whatever it means to "be religious" or have attempted to measure religiosity by using unidimensional indicators such as church attendance or religious affiliation. Recently, however, there has been increased concern as to what comprises an adequate measure of religiosity. Today, most researchers would agree that the use of a single criterion to provide an accurate reflection of the concept covers too broad an area to be considered meaningful (Vernon, 1962). In directing attention to the development of more adequate measures of religiosity, many scholars have conceptualized religious commitment as multidimensional (see, for example: Glock, 1962; Fukuyama, 1960; Lenski, 1963; Faulkner and DeJong, 1966; King, 1967; Broen, 1957; Cardwell, 1969; Allen and Hites, 1961; and Cline and Richards, 1965). In this regard, Glock (1962) is credited with developing the initial formalized definition of religious commitment as a multidimensional concept. Glock correctly perceived the problem in the measurement of religiosity, stating that:

> A first and obvious requirement if religious
> commitment is to be comprehensively assessed
> is to establish the different ways in which
> individuals can be religious. With some few
> exceptions, past research has curiously avoided

37

this fundamental question (italics in original).

In an initial attempt to deal with the problem of measuring religion, Glock (1962) conceptualized five dimensions of religiosity. These dimensions he defined as the experiential, ideological, ritualistic, intellectual, and consequential. He concluded his work by indicating the need for research into the possible configuration(s) of the dimensions.

As is apparent when one surveys the literature, Glock's work has generated a significant amount of research in the area of the measurement of religious commitment. Curiously, however, the empirical investigations which have been launched as a result of Glock's efforts have apparently overlooked a warning he presented in his conceptual framework (of those who have neglected this warning, the present author is equally guilty). Glock (1962) advised, "Nor can we assume that religiosity expressed on one dimension automatically assures its being menifested on other dimensions as well." In a later statement concerning the identical problem, Glock and Stark (1965:22) again set forth the same theoretical possibility:

> It is scarcely plausible that the various mani festations of religiosity are entirely independent of each other. However, several recent studies strongly suggest that being religious on one dimension does not necessarily imply religiosity on other dimensions. Fukuyama found, using a sample of Congregationalists, that those who scored high on ritual observance and biblical literacy tended to score low on religious belief and religious feeling, and vice versa.

In view of such advice, it is surprising to find such statements as "Hypothetically, a positive relationship would be expected among the five dimensions," and "That these dimensions are positively related is indeed what one would anticipate" (Faulkner and DeJong, 1966), in research which is concerned with development of a multidimensional measure of religiosity. It is also interesting to note that some authors (Ludwig and Blank, 1969), while recognizing the theoretical possibility of an inverse relationship between scales for some religious types, suggest only a positive relationship between the extremes of commitment, i.e., the "non-religious" and pervasive-religious." This is especially relevant in terms of Vernon's (1968) finding that the category "religious nones" evidences variability in religious commitment scores. This finding would suggest, it is contended, that not all religious nones would score low on all scales of religiosity.

While agreeing with the above statement by Glock (1962) and Glock and Stark (1965), a further position is taken, which is believed to be consistent with Glock. It is contended that items which scale for one denomination or religious body do not, a priori, yield the same scale for another denomination or religious body. It is believed further that there are sufficient data at hand to support such a contention. Essentially the question being asked is can we accept the assumption that Catholics, Jews, Presbyterians, and Baptists have the same criteria for commitment? Religion may mean something quite different to each category. Certainly each of these is woven into the societal fabric in quite different ways.

When one denominational group is examined and the multidimensionality of religious commitment is verified, researchers have apparently assumed that comprehensive measures of religious commitment across denominations have been derived. This paper does not necessarily disagree, but takes the position that the research thus far conducted does not suggest that such is the case. It is the contention, instead, that the data indicate that up to this point, comprehensive measures across denominations have not been developed.

In order to illustrate the contention being made, data collected by Faulkner and DeJong (1966) are presented in intercorrelation matrix form, comparing one denomination with another denomination for correlations among the five dimensions of religiosity.[1] These data are presented in Table 1.[2]

An examination of the intercorrelations among the five dimensions suggests that Faulkner and DeJong have constructed a multidimensional scale of religiosity that measures Catholic-like religious commitment. Comparing Catholics with Lutherans, we observe that all of the intercorrelations for Catholics are statistically significant at the .05 level. For Lutherans, however, the following intercorrelations are not significant: ideological/ritualistic, ideological/experiential, ideological/consequential, intellectual/experiential, ritualistic/experiential, and experiential/consequential. This does not suggest that these dimensions do not exist for Lutherans. The correlations that are not significant do suggest, it is contended, that these dimensions do not exist

	Lutheran (n=160)						Jewish (n=37)			
	1	2	3	4	5		1	2	3	4	5
C 1	X	.50	.25[a]	.09[a]	.19[a]	C 1	X	.32	.57	.33	-.11[a]
A T 2	.48	X	.32	.25[a]	.49	A T 2	.48	X	.28[a]	.45	.24[a]
H O 3	.45	.41	X	.11[a]	.41	H O 3	.45	.41	X	.38	.07[a]
L I 4	.42	.46	.32	X	.14[a]	L I 4	.42	.46	.32	X	.18[a]
C 5	.43	.35	.47	.33	X	C 5	.43	.35	.47	.33	X

	Presbyterian (n=44)						Lutheran (n=160)			
	1	2	3	4	5		1	2	3	4	5
C 1	X	.52	.47	.45	.28[a]	P 1	X	.50	.25[a]	.09[a]	.19[a]
A T 2	.48	X	.52	.46	.13[a]	R E 2	.52	X	.32	.25[a]	.49
H O 3	.45	.41	X	.24[a]	.25[a]	S B 3	.47	.52	X	.11[a]	.41
L I 4	.42	.46	.32	X	.21[a]	Y. 4	.45	.46	.24[a]	X	.14[a]
C 5	.43	.35	.47	.33	X	5	.28[a]	.13[a]	.25[a]	.21[a]	X

	Lutheran (n=160)						Jewish (n=37)			
	1	2	3	4	5		1	2	3	4	5
1	X	.50	.25[a]	.09[a]	.19[a]	P 1	X	.32	.57	.33	-.11[a]
J E 2	.32	X	.32	.25[a]	.49	R E 2	.52	X	.28[a]	.45	.24[a]
W I 3	.57	.28[a]	X	.11[a]	.41	S B 3	.47	.52	X	.38	.07[a]
S H 4	.33	.45	.38	X	.14[a]	Y. 4	.45	.46	.24[a]	X	.18[a]
5	.11[a]	.24[a]	.07[a]	.18[a]	X	5	.28[a]	.13[a]	.25[a]	.21[a]	X

SOURCE: Joseph E. Faulkner and G. F. DeJong, 1966. "Religiosity in 5-D: An Empirical Analysis." Social Forces, 45 (December, 246-254.
 a.=Not significant at .05 level 3 =ritualistic dimension
 1 =ideological dimension 4 =experiential dimension
 2 =intellectual dimension 5 =consequential dimension

in the same manner for Lutherans as they do for Catholics--
i.e., the content of some of the dimensions is different for
Lutherans. These same results can be found to be true for
Catholic/Jewish, Catholic/Presbyterian, Lutheran/Presbyterian,
Lutheran/Jewish, and Jewish/Presbyterian comparisons. The
correlations that do not agree for the above comparisons are
presented in Table 2.

TABLE 2
INTERFAITH MULTIDIMENSIONAL CORRELATIONS
NOT AGREEING[a]

Denominations Compared	Intercorrelations Not Agreeing						
Catholic-Lutheran	r_{13}	r_{14}	r_{15}	r_{24}	r_{34}	r_{45}	
Catholic-Jewish	r_{15}	r_{23}	r_{25}	r_{35}	r_{45}		
Catholic-Presbyterian	r_{15}	r_{25}	r_{34}	r_{35}	r_{45}		
Lutheran-Presbyterian	r_{13}	r_{14}	r_{24}	r_{25}	r_{35}		
Lutheran-Jewish	r_{13}	r_{14}	r_{23}	r_{24}	r_{25}	r_{34}	r_{35}
Jewish-Presbyterian	r_{23}	r_{34}					

SOURCE: Joseph E. Faulkner and G. F. DeJong, 1966.
"Religiosity in 5-D: An Empirical Analysis." Social Forces,
45 (December), 246-254.
a. Disagreement is indicated by one significant and one not
significant correlation being compared.

The question of why any two dimensions should be statistically correlated for any denomination should, of course,
be asked. Consistent with the conceptual development of
Glock (1962), there is no completely logical reason to expect that any two dimensions would be statistically correlated, either positively or negatively. In Glock's words,
nothing "assures" a correlation in either direction. However, that is not the point of contention in question here.

Apparently, researchers have developed scales of religious commitment, while accepting, implicitly or explicitly, the notion that is is possible for the relationship between any two scales to be inverse (see Cardwell, 1969, for an explicit statement of this possibility). The problem arises, however, when a scale of religious commitment developed for one religious group is applied across denominations to other religious groups (again, see Cardwell, 1969).

It is true that if the scales were found to be orthogonal via factor analysis that a correlation would not be expected between the various dimensions. Again, however, if five scales were found to be orthogonal for Catholics it could not, it is contended, be <u>assumed</u> that the scales were orthogonal in the same manner for other denominations. What is being suggested is that a series of items which form five orthogonal dimensions for one religious group may combine or fail to have sufficiently high loadings and, therefore, form only two or three orthogonal dimensions for another religious group. It is possible, in other words, that there may be between dimension shifts of items, if the same items are factored, when they are applied across denominations. A further consideration is that one measure of religious commitment, even if the same for all denominations may have differential predictability in terms of some dependent variable. The Faulkner and DeJong (1966) data at least suggest that these outcomes are a distinct possibility.

Perhaps the striking aspect of these data is that Faulkner and DeJong apparently have devised an adequate measure of multidimensional Catholic-like commitment. This is illustrated in Table 3. As is discernible from Table 3 all ten of the possible intercorrelations among the religiosity subscales are significant for Catholics. For the Presbyterian and Jewish groups, there are five significant (although not the same five for either group), and for Lutherans, four of the intercorrelations are significant, while six of them are not. This is not unexpected when we consider an earlier warning by Glock and Stark (1965: 23):

> It would ease the burden of analysis and research if each of the core dimensions delineated above could be assumed to be itself unilateral. Such an assumption would allow us to ignore the questions of sub-dimensions and to move directly to discussing ways of distinguishing more religious people from less religious ones. Unfortunately, the matter is not so

simple. Within every dimension it is necessary to make distinctions in kind as well as degree.

Correlations Between Dimensions	Catholic	Lutheran	Presbyterian	Jewish
1 and 2	S	S	S	S
1 and 3	S	NS	S	S
1 and 4	S	NS	S	S
1 and 5	S	NS	NS	NS
2 and 3	S	S	S	NS
2 and 4	S	NS	S	S
2 and 5	S	S	NS	NS
3 and 4	S	NS	NS	S
3 and 5	S	S	NS	NS
4 and 5	S	NS	NS	NS

S=significant at .05; NS=not significant at .05.
Catholic: S=10/NS=0
Lutheran: S= 4/NS=6
Presbyterian: S= 5/NS=5
Jewish: S= 5/NS=5

SOURCE: Joseph E. Faulkner and G. F. DeJong. 1966. "Religiosity in 5-D: An Empirical Analysis." Social Forces, 45 (December), 246-254.

Thus, there seems to be reason to question whether we can develop one measure of commitment which will work across denominations.[3] Denominational comparisons could be made, however, if for each major denomination (or other category for that matter--i.e., the "new denominationalism") we could measure how well each respondent (or group of respondents) measured up to some denomination-specific criteria. This would tell us how well Jews measure up to Jewish criteria (in which attendance is deemphasized), and how well Catholics measure up to Catholic criteria (in which attendance is emphasized). It is possible that an individual (or group of individuals) is a member of one denomination which emphasizes ritual acts as a means to salvation (e.g., Episcopalians) but scores low on a ritualism scale while scoring high on a supernaturalism scale. This would, according to evidence supplied by Glock and Stark (1965: ch. 5), indicate religious commitment more closely akin to the Southern Baptist denomination than the Episcopal denomination. That such an outcome is possible has been given support by Finner (forthcoming). Studying the utility of religious "preference" and "membership" in determining religious affiliation. Finner related both preference and membership to religious commitment and concluded that religious preference has a stronger relationship to religiosity than does actual membership. It is possible, therefore, that if denomination-specific criteria were used in scales of religiosity, individuals who are low in terms of commitment within the denomination to which they belong may be high in terms of some other denomination-specific commitment measure. Denominational comparisons could be made if some such pattern was followed. Using the approach outlined herein, would permit us to categorize various groups in a new (or at least another) manner. We could distinguish, for example, Catholic-like from Jewish or Baptist-like groups, and so on, regardless of what the formal name of the denomination was.

The data presented here suggest that the multidimensional measures within denominations may yield more satisfactory results than measures across denominations. These data support King's (1967) contention:

> The multidimensional hypothesis should be retested with greater rigor on a number of different, and larger populations. Subjects should be drawn from a variety of religious backgrounds (Jewish as well as Christian) and from a variety of socio-cultural areas (within and outside the United States).

Research designed to reject or verify the hypothesis that different measures of religious commitment should be derived for different denominational groupings should be conducted prior to making statements concerning comprehensive measures of interfaith commitment.

FOOTNOTES AND REFERENCES CITED

1. These data are taken from Faulkner and DeJong (1966:250). Intercorrelations were not included for two of the groups examined by Faulkner and DeJong because they represent the combining of denominational groups (Methodist and E.U.B., and Episcopal and Church of Christ), which is the point of contention in this paper. It should also be pointed out that this paper does not represent a criticism

of Faulkner and DeJong, especially in the sense outlined by Weigert and Thomas (1969). On the issues outlined by Weigert and Thomas, the author is in agreement with the rejoinder of Faulkner and DeJong (1969).

2. Correlation coefficients are presented in the same sense as that of Faulkner and DeJong (1966:250).

3. The comments that follow are indebted to the advice and consultation of Professor Glenn M. Vernon of the University of Utah and Professor Stephen L. Finner of the University of Delaware. Any misinterpretation of their advice is, of course, my responsibility.

Allen, Edmund E. and R. W. Hites
    1961 "Factors in religious attitudes of older adolescents."
        J. of Social Psychology 55: 265-273.

Broen, William E., Jr.
    1957 "A factor-analytic study of religious attitudes."
        J. of Abnormal Psychology 54: 176-179.

Cardwell, Jerry D.
    1969 "The relationship between religious commitment and
        pre-marital sexual permissiveness: a five-dimensional
        analysis." Soc. Analysis 30 (Summer): 72-80.

Cline, Victor B. and J. M. Richards, Jr.
    1965 "A factor-analytic study of religious belief and
        behavior." J. of Personality and Social Psychology
        1: 569-578.

Faulkner, Joseph E. and G. F. DeJong
    1966 "Religiosity in 5-D: an empirical analysis." Social
        Forces 45 (December): 246-254.

    1969 "On measuring the religious variable: rejoinder to
        Weigert and Thomas." Social Forces 48 (December):
        263-267

Finner, Stephen L., forthcoming
        "Religious membership and religious preference: equal
        indicators of religiosity?" J. for the Scientific
        Study of Religion.

Fukuyama, Yoshio
    1960 "The major dimensions of church membership." Rev. of
        Religious Research 2: 154-161.

Glock, Charles Y.
  1962 "On the study of religious commitment." Religious
        Education Research Supplement (July-August):
        S98-S110.

--- and Rodney Stark
  1965 Religion and Society in Tension. New York:
        Rand McNally.

King, Morton
  1967 "Measuring the religious variable: nine proposed
        dimensions." J. for the Scientific Study of
        Religion 6: 173-190.

Lenski, Gerhard
  1963 The Religious Factor: A Sociological Study of
        Religion's Impact on Politics, Economics, and
        Family Life. Garden City: Doubleday.'

Ludwig, David J. and Thomas Blank
  1969 "Measurement of religion as a perpetual set." J.
        for the Scientific Study of Religion 8: 319-321.

Vernon, Glenn M.
  1962 The Sociology of Religion. New York: McGraw-Hill.
  1968 "The religious nones: a neglected category." J.
        for the Scientific Study of Religion 7: 219-229.

Weigert, A. J. and D. A. Thomas
  1969 "Religiosity in 5-D: a critical note." Social
        Forces 48 (December): 260-263.

* Reprinted from Pacific Sociological Review, 14 (Jan), 1971,
79-88, with permission.

INTERFAITH COMPARISON OF MULTIDIMENSIONAL MEASURES OF RELIGIOSITY

David L. Klemmack and Jerry D. Cardwell*

Recently, largely due to the seminal article of Glock (1962), researchers have explored the multidimensionality of religious commitment (see, for example, Allen and Hites, 1961; Broen, 1957; Cardwell, 1969; Cline and Richards, 1965; Faulkner and DeJong, 1966; Finner and Gamache, 1969; Fukuyama, 1961; King, 1967; Lenski, 1963). This paper proceeds from the proposition that religious commitment is indeed multidimensional, posing, as suggested by Glock (1962), the additional question of whether it is necessary to make distinctions of kind as well as degree when developing scales designed to measure interfaith commitment. While researchers have verified the multidimensionality of religiosity, it remains problematic whether the resulting measures apply equally across denominations. Religion and, subsequently, religiosity may mean something quite different for different denominational categories. The problem of the paper is to determine the extent to which multidimensional measures of commitment developed for each of various denominations are comparable.

The position taken by Glock (1962) is that each religious denomination emphasizes to some degree five different dimensions of commitment (religious belief, religious effects, religious behavior, religious knowledge, and religious feelings). This article brings forth another point which has largely been ignored by the research stimulated by Glock: that the manifestation of each dimension of commitment may vary among denominations. Specifically, the socialization experiences of the individual probably vary between specific denominations, leading to a somewhat different definition of religious commitment dependent on the denomination. Abstract Christian theology as elaborated by such theologians as Calvin, Luther, and Wesley is not presented to the lay members of any congregation. Therefore the salient factors of the individual's religious commitment will more appropriately lie in the area identified by Luckmann (1967) as "church religion." Specifically, the critical features of religious commitment lie not in theological considerations, but in the more particularistic aspects of the denomination: the guidelines for appropriate beliefs and behavior as they are translated from the more general theological teachings of the church. Thus, theology is relevant to the members of the different denominations only as it is translated into terms of what they are expected to believe, the ritual they are expected to follow, and the guidelines presented for everyday activity. The position taken in this paper is that religious commitment varies among religious denominations as a function of the differential importance placed on belief structures, ritual acts, and permissible secular activities by the various denominations.

The initial assumption is that the degree of religious commitment with respect to any particular dimension causes variation in the indicants of that dimension as a direct function of the strength of the individual's commitment. Therefore, to say that any given dimension of commitment has the same meaning for a variety of religious denominations implies that the factor loadings (correlation between item and underlying factor) should be approximately equivalent across religious denominations for all items assumed to measure that dimension. The particular situation under consideration in this paper, however, is somewhat more complex.

Since religiosity is assumed to be multidimensional, the possibility exists that any given item may be a function of some set of dimensions of commitment or other unidentified concepts (residual variables) rather than being factorially pure. This suggests two additional conditions to be met before the conclusion can be made that multidimensional

48

measures of commitment are comparable across denominations. Not only must the factor loading for any given item be similar across denominations, but also the same items must define the same factor space for each of the denominations. For example, if a given set of items defines a four-dimensional space for one group, it must also define a four-dimensional space for another group. Failure to find this condition indicates that the structure of commitment varies between the two groups. Even this, however, is insufficient to define parallel structure of commitment. Any item may be viewed as a function of a set of underlying concepts (religious belief, religious effects, and religious ritualism in this study). If the structure of the factor loadings (the path coefficients from underlying concept to specific item) varies among religious denominations, it is possible to conclude that the structure of commitment itself varies.[1] Lack of comparability among factor loadings among religious denominations implies that the response set of the individual is denominationally specific.

To summarize, religiosity and its various dimensions are parallel among denominations if and only if the separate factor matrices are equivalent. This, of course, represents a necessary but not sufficient condition for the conclusion that religiosity has the same meaning for different religious denominations. Failure to find equivalent factor matrices, however, strongly suggests that the meaning of commitment is variable.

DATA COLLECTION

The data for this study were collected from students who met the double criteria of enrollment in at least one of a selected set of sociology courses and attendance at class on the day the questionnaire was administered. All of the students attended a medium-sized (student population approximately 11,000), land-grant college in the southeastern United States. Of the 277 students from whom data were collected, the majority (199) were male.

All of the students were requested to indicate whether they were a member of a church and, if so, what particular religious affiliation the church represented. The specific groups used in the analysis were Catholics (n = 39), Baptists (n = 37), Methodists (n = 64), and nonaffiliates (n = 55).[2] The remaining 72 cases were spread throughout a variety of other

49

religious affiliations and were excluded from further analysis.

A set of 23 Likert format items assumed in their totality to reflect three of the five dimensions of religiosity suggested by Glock (1962) was developed (see Table 1 for a more complete description of the items). All but five of the items (frequency of nightly prayer, grace at meals, and three items referring specifically to participation in youth activities) have been used in previous studies of religious commitment (Faulkner and DeJong, 1966; Cardwell, 1969; Finner and Gamache, 1969). Seven of the items were assumed to reflect the religious belief or ideological dimension and included such questions as "How frequently, in the last month, have you attended the regularly scheduled Sabbath meetings of a church?" The final five items were assumed to reflect the religious effects or consequential dimension and included such questions as "Is it morally acceptable for a Christian businessman, if he so desires, to keep his furniture store open for business on Sunday?"[3]

A correlation matrix of the 23 items designed to measure the various dimensions of religious commitment was obtained for each of the four groups, (Catholics, Baptists, Methodists, and nonaffiliates).[4] Each of the matrices was then factored using a principal-factor solution with squared multiple correlations as estimates of the variable communalities. Kaiser's criterion was used as an index of the completeness of factorization and the resulting matrices were rotated to "meaningfulness" utilizing a varimax rotation (Harmon, 1967).[5]

RESULTS AND DISCUSSION

Examination of Table 1 indicates that important similarities exist among the four factor matrices. All four matrices appear to have four factors in common, although the order in which the factors appear varies from solution to solution. The first factor identified appears to reflect the religious belief dimension. In general, the seven items assumed to reflect religious belief load highly on this factor, while the remaining items, with some exceptions, do not. Also, the belief items have generally low loadings on the remaining factors.[6]

The second factor identified reflects a religious effects or consequences dimension. Two of the five items assumed to measure effects, those concerning the operation of commercial enterprises on the Sabbath, load heavily on one factor of each group though not necessarily the same factor for all five groups. The remaining three items assumed to reflect religious effects had no consistent pattern of loadings among the denominations.

The final two factors identified for all of the groups involve the ritualism items. Typically, religious ritualism or religious behavior has been measured by items which reflect adult church attendance, contributions, and the like. Since, however, the sample used in this study consisted of college students, items which reflected participation in the more youth-oriented groups usually found on the campuses were included with the traditional indicators of ritualism. Since the youth-oriented items paralleled those typically considered to measure ritualism, it was assumed that they would also load on a general ritualism factor. The results of the factor analysis indicate that this assumption was not well founded. The ritualism items defined two separate factors for all four groups. The first centered around the items dealing with youth activities (attend Sunday School, member of youth groups, attend youth groups) and was labeled youth ritualism. The second factor centered on the items typically used to measure ritualism, particularly those reflecting financial contributions and average yearly attendance, and was labeled adult ritualism. Apparently the two types of participation (youth and adult) reflect a difference in kind and not degree of ritualism, thus supporting Glock's (1962) suggestion that both substantive and procedural problems may be met in an attempt to conceptualize religiosity.

To briefly review the findings thus far, it appears that the appropriate causal structure underlying the four factor matrices consists of four different concepts or types of religious commitment: religious belief, religious effects, youth ritualism, and adult ritualism. The matrices provide additional information suggesting that the causal link between concept and item varies among religious affiliations. A cursory examination of the factor matrices for Baptists and Catholics indicates that they consist of five rather than four factors. Thus, it is possible to conclude, at minimum, that the conceptual base of the set of items varies somewhat from religious group to religious group. The remainder of this paper deals with the isolation and explanation of the differences in the structure of religious commitment as it varies among religious affiliations.

51

TABLE 1

FACTOR MATRICES OF RELIGIOUS COMMITMENT ITEMS FOR FOUR GROUPS

		Methodists				Baptists			
	IVa	I	II	III	I	II	III	IV	V
Belief									
(3) Virgin Birth[b]	.48	.49	.20	.18	.69	.00	.02	.20	.23
(7) God	.44	.60	.01	.18	.60	.11	.18	.55	.08
(9) End of World	.67	.52	.08	.14	.78	.06	.29	.27	.18
(14) Jesus	.34	.49	.04	.44	.63	.09	.23	.52	.19
(17) Life After Death	.61	.40	.20	.16	.81	.11	-.14	.06	.06
(19) Repentence	.55	.29	.27	.27	.88	.08	.10	-.07	.14
(23) Bible	.50	.11	.12	.36	.38	.02	.29	.52	.29
Ritualism									
(1) Attend/Month	.21	.26	.44	.69	.38	.51	-.13	.14	.57
(2) Contribute	.11	.02	.27	.67	.06	.01	.30	.11	.75
(4) Active	.19	.34	.53	.49	.22	.54	.49	.03	.36
(5) Sunday School Attend	.62	.10	.36	.23	.35	.64	-.27	.07	.44
(8) Nightly Prayer	.47	.24	.09	.24	.63	.14	.17	.39	.01
(10) Youthgroup Member	.14	.04	.80	.17	-.15	.78	.16	.17	.15
(11) Youthgroup Attend	.06	.15	.90	.20	-.01	.83	.05	.20	.05
(13) Church Work	.41	.03	.57	.27	.34	.76	.23	-.06	.18
(15) Grace	.38	.24	.02	.43	.32	.49	.40	.03	.22
(18) Attend/Year	.21	.14	.17	.86	.30	.32	.22	.22	.66
(21) Active/Friends	.31	.18	.35	.55	.43	.39	.60	.12	.26
Effects									
(6) Moderate Drinking	.18	.60	.05	.16	.18	.05	.17	.13	.66
(16) Gambling	.35	.40	.09	.23	.34	.21	-.13	.37	.43
(20) Divorce	.65	.23	.25	.03	.00	.13	.80	.15	.19
(22) Christian Business/Sunday	.13	.77	.04	.13	.24	.44	.15	.61	.17
(24) Jewish Business/Sunday	.06	.65	.32	.06	.07	.15	-.10	.76	.15

TABLE 1 (Continued)

	Catholics					Non-affiliates			
	Ia	V	II	III	IV	I	II	III	IV
Belief									
(3) Virgin Birthb	.40	.20	.39	.24	.55	.81	.11	.09	.21
(7) God	.81	.03	.09	.42	.08	.87	.03	.11	.18
(9) End of World	.61	-.06	.13	.43	.41	.81	.19	.19	.16
(14) Jesus	.85	.06	.12	.19	.23	.91	.02	.03	.16
(17) Life After Death	.64	.12	.11	.16	.30	.68	.14	.18	.17
(19) Repentence	.49	.00	.27	.14	.25	.67	.18	.26	.16
(23) Bible	.82	.12	-.04	.14	.16	.59	-.04	.32	.20
Ritualism									
(1) Attend/Month	.36	.22	.21	.59	.24	.21	.38	-.02	.67
(2) Contribute	.19	-.06	-.08	.69	.36	.17	-.05	.19	.87
(4) Active	.21	.17	.17	.82	.18	.20	.30	.04	.78
(5) Sunday School Attend	.03	.21	-.04	.09	.32	.15	.40	.01	.37
(8) Nightly Prayer	.26	.11	-.00	.68	-.11	.56	.22	.06	.26
(10) Youthgroup Member	.06	.38	.21	.12	.09	.07	.90	-.09	.54
(11) Youthgroup Attend	.09	.99	.13	-.00	.08	.15	.40	.01	.37
(13) Church Work	-.06	.02	.17	.51	-.03	.11	-.04	.012	.08
(15) Grace	.22	-.04	.06	.27	.45	.21	-.15	.65	.24
(18) Attend/Year	.35	.10	.32	.59	.37	.27	.10	-.02	.66
(21) Active/Friends	.24	.47	.22	.44	.04	.30	.07	.07	.42
Effects									
(6) Moderate Drinking	.64	.20	.08	-.05	-.25	.12	.58	.22	-.02
(16) Gambling	.06	.04	.28	-.00	.06	.42	.46	.50	.21
(20) Divorce	.26	.01	.05	.06	.64	.58	.13	.29	.11
(22) Christian Business/Sunday	.13	.16	.77	.26	.20	.06	.22	.78	-.11
(24) Jewish Business/Sunday	.03	.15	.90	.20	-.07	.22	.14	.71	-.07

a. Roman numeral refers to the order in which the factor appears in the rotated solution. For convenience, the factors are re-ordered in the following manner: belief, youth ritualism, effects, adult ritualism, non-common. b. The number at the start of each item refers order in which item appears in religiosity section of questionnaire.

53

The structure of commitment is five-dimensional for both Baptists and Catholics, while four-dimensional for the remaining two groups, a finding not surprising from the standpoint of the general dominance of these two churches. Since they are larger than the others, they probably command greater resources enabling them to better communicate with members. This suggests the hypothesis that the greater the communication input to the individual about his religion, the more complex he perceives his religion to be and, subsequently, the more complex the structure of his commitment, when complexity is taken to mean the number of different ideas to which the individual is exposed. This, however, is only one possible explanation for the differences in the dimensionality of commitment among the four denominations under consideration. The critical point is that the results provide evidence suggesting that the conceptual structure of commitment is variable.

Although Baptists and Catholics are similar in that the responses of both groups define five rather than four factors, the nature of the fifth factor varies somewhat between the two denominations. Two items, attitude toward divorce and grace at meals, load on the noncommon factor for both Baptists and Catholics, but here the similarity ends. The two remaining items which define the factor for Baptists (self-definition of extent of participation in church activities and self-definition of extent of participation relative to that of friends) reflect the individual's perception of his activity, while the items defining the factor for Catholics (extent of belief in the Virgin Birth and extent of belief in the revelation of the world's end) reflect religious belief. Thus, although the structure of religiosity is similar for Baptists and Catholics, the particularistic aspects of commitment are not. The noncommon factor which separates these two denominations from the others has a somewhat different content depending on the denomination considered.

Although communalities in the remaining factors (religious belief, religious effects, youth ritualism, and adult ritualism) exist for all four groups, there are also striking dissimilarities. For example, an examination of the items assumed to measure religious effects indicates that only two, Christian businessman opening on Sunday and Jewish businessman opening on Sunday, load consistently on the same factor for all groups. (At the same time, two items-- gambling and divorce--load on the belief dimension for nonaffiliates and Methodists, suggesting that belief is more broadly conceived for these two groups than for the remaining two.)[7]

Examination of the items assumed to reflect youth and adult ritualism indicates a striking difference between Protestants on the one hand and Catholics and nonaffiliates on the other. Apparently Catholics and nonaffiliates responded to the ritualism items from an adult rather than a youth perspective. Only two of the ritualism items for Catholics and three for nonaffiliates had substantial loadings on the youth dimension. Conversely, many of the items loaded solely on the adult dimension, suggesting that adult ritualism is a general and youth ritualism a specific concept for these two religious categories. The Protestant groups, on the other hand, appeared to respond from a youth perspective. From six to eight items, depending on the specific Protestant denomination under consideration, had relatively high loadings on the youth ritualism dimension. Furthermore, few items loaded solely on the adult ritualism factor.

The explanation for the differences in the two patterns probably lies in the nature of the church experience to which the individual is exposed. Protestant churches have emphasized the concepts of peer relations and youth fellowship, and have typically provided situations in which peer group relations have had an opportunity to develop. The Catholic church, on the other hand, stresses adult ritualistic behavior such as "confession" even for the very young. This, in turn, probably leads to increased importance in more adult-like activities.

Even though the pattern of loadings for nonaffiliates resembles that of Catholics, its explanation is probably different. It is likely that nonaffiliates are not given the opportunity for membership in youth-oriented church groups and that such circumstances preclude the youth response from the attitudinal position they occupy. Thus, the emphasis on adult ritualism for this group is not surprising.

Another type of pattern occurs among the items assumed to measure religious belief. The critical factor in considering this dimension is not how many items load for any given group, but on which factors the items load. All of the belief items for all four groups have substantial loadings on the belief factor, but some items also have substantial loadings on other factors as well. In general, for the two

Protestant groups, some belief items also load on the adult ritualism dimension. However, for nonaffiliates, the belief items load only on the belief dimension.

The differences in the pattern of loadings among the groups can be conceived of as a function of the theological differences among the religions as they are communicated to lay individuals. People claiming to be of one religious affiliation probably respond to items assumed to be measuring belief from a different set than those claiming another affiliation. More specifically, a church, operating through some designated functionary such as a minister or priest, communicates information concerning the relationship expected between belief in the particular content emphasized varies somewhat among denominations and is probably a function of differing theologies.[8] In any case, belief is confounded with other dimensions of religiosity. The critical point of this article resides in the comparability of multidimensional measures of commitment among various denominations. The results indicate, at least in a tentative sense, that the particular manifestation of each dimension of commitment varies among the denominations considered. However, important differences in the interpretation of the dimensions also exist. Belief for the Protestant is not the same as belief for the Catholic because the items assumed to measure belief for Protestants are confounded with effects. Apparently the Protestant, when considering belief, also considers its effects on his behavior, while the Catholic considers it relative to the rituals of the church. When considering the ritualism dimension, the case is even clearer. Adult ritualism for Catholics encompasses a much broader range of behaviors than it does for Protestants. However, youth ritualism is a much broader concept for Protestants than for Catholics.

Although the particular sampling procedures utilized and the minimal number of cases upon which the analyses were based severely limit the generalizability of the conclusions, the findings do make intuitive sense. It seems unreasonable to assume that belief, ritualism, effects, or any of the other dimensions of religiosity are equivalent from denomination to denomination. All religious groups emphasize some aspects of religiosity more than others, giving those emphasized a broader, richer meaning. At the same time, the particular aspects emphasized vary among denominations, for, if they did not, all denominations would be equivalent. Naturally, important similarities exist among denominations, and it is critical to isolate these as well. However, such similarities are problematic. The researcher, rather than assuming a parallel structure of religiosity, would be well advised to demonstrate it empirically.

FOOTNOTES AND REFERENCES

1. Blalock (1969, 1968) and Turner and Stevens (1959) suggest that factor loadings are simply path coefficients from an underlying concept to measures of the concept. Variability in measures is then conceptualized as being a function of variability in the underlying concept and high path coefficients imply high determination in a standardized system.

2. The number of cases for any given denomination is inadequate for definitive analysis. However, consistency in the results may, in part, counteract this inadequacy. Failure to find meaningful patterns, however, can be a function of the large sampling error involved when using small numbers of cases.

3. Copies of the complete questionnaire are available upon request from the authors.

4. The matrix of Pearsonian r's was based upon the N_{ij} observations where N_{ij} is the number of individuals responding to the ith and j^{th} items jointly under the assumption that the best estimate of rho is r based on all available data. This implies that failure to respond to a given item is a function of random causes.

5. Strictly speaking, a factor is defined by the linear combination of factor loadings across items. Thus, the most appropriate means of comparison for two factors is the degree of correlation between factor scores derived from the two factors. Since, however, different individuals are involved in each case, such a procedure is impossible with this study. Instead, the position taken is that if the linear composition of an item varies from matrix to matrix, the response to that item is a function of a different causal set. To the extent that this occurs consistently across items, the factor matrices are not comparable. This condition occurs only when the correlation matrices, aside from sampling error, are not comparable. Consistency of results is emphasized, in

57

that no convenient index of sampling error of the factor matrix is presently available, and small differences between corresponding factor loadings are ignored for much the same reason.

6. Factor loadings with an absolute value of approximately .4 and above are considered large for the purposes of this study.

7. Breadth of a factor here refers simply to the number of different items having high loadings on a given factor. A high breadth factor is one on which many items have high loadings, while a low breadth factor is one on which few items have high loadings.

8. Naturally, religions differ in other respects besides their theologies. More importantly, the individuals of one particular religious affiliation differ from those of another in a variety of characteristics such as socioeconomic status. Possibly differences in lay congregations are a function of individual self-selection in which the individual selects a church based on a perceived compatability of theological teaching and personal beliefs. The consequence, for whatever the reason, is that belief takes on a somewhat different dependent upon the affiliation of the individual

Allen, E. E. and R. W. Hites
  1961 "Factors in religious attitudes of older adolescents." J. of Social Psychology 55: 265-273.

Blalock, Hubert M., Jr.
  1968 "The measurement problem: a gap between the languages of theory and research." Pp. 5-27 in H. M. Blalock, Jr., and A. B. Blalock (eds.) Methodology in Social Research. New York: McGraw-Hill.

  1969 Theory Construction: From Verbal to Mathematical Formulations. Englewood Cliffs, N.J.: Prentice-Hall.

Broen, William E., Jr.
  1957 "A factor-analytic study of religious attitudes." J. of Abnormal Psychology 54: 176-179.

Cardwell, J. D.
  1969 "The relationship between religious commitment and premarital sexual permissiveness: a 5-D analysis." Soc. Analysis 30 (Summer): 72-80.

Cline, V. B. and J. M. Richards, Jr.
  1965 "A factor-analytic study of religious belief and
        behavior." J. of Personality and Social Psychology
        1: 569-578.

Faulkner, J. E. and G. F. DeJong
  1966 "Religiosity in 5-D: an empirical analysis." Social
        Forces 45 (December): 246-254.

Finner, Stephen L. and Jerome D. Gamache
  1969 "The relation between religious commitment and atti-
        tudes toward induced abortion." Soc. Analysis 30
        (Spring): 1-12.

Fukuyama, Yoshio
  1961 "The major dimensions of church membership." Rev.
        of Religious Research 2: 154-161.

Glock, C. Y.
  1962 "On the study of religious commitment." Religious
        Education (Research Supplement) 42 (July/August):
        98-110.

Harmon, Harry H.
  1967 Modern Factor Analysis. Chicago: Univ. of Chicago
        Press.

King, Morton
  1967 "Measuring the religious variable: nine proposed
        dimensions." J. for Scientific Study of Religion 6:
        173-190.

Lenski, Gerhard
  1963 The Religious Factor, Garden City, N.Y.: Doubleday.

Luckmann, Thomas
  1967 The Invisible Religion, New York: Macmillan.

Turner, Malcom E. and Charles D. Stevens
  1959 "The regression analysis of causal paths." Biometrics
        15 (June): 236-258.

* Reprinted from Pacific Sociological Review, Vol. 16, No. 4
(October), 1973, 495-507, with permission.

DENOMINATIONAL UNITY OF SOUTHERN BAPTIST SEMINARY STUDENTS*

Jerry D. Cardwell and Thomas Ward

The purpose of this study is to investigate the possibility of dissension among the prospective clergy of a Protestant denomination--specifically, the Southern Baptists. Attention is centered on attitudes toward the interpretation of scripture, and belief in the traditional doctrine of the church. Earlier research--which has primarily been concerned with the "ecumenical movement"--has suggested that disagreement does occur among both Protestant laity (Glock and Stark: 1967), and Protestant clergy (Hadden: 1967). Although the studies by Glock and Stark, and Hadden, were designed to investigate the sources of the ecumenical movement, their data suggest that an investigation into the nature of denominational unity would prove both interesting and useful when attempting to explain such matters as the strength of the church in contemporary society. Unlike previous studies which investigated the laity and clergy, this study samples a different population--the potential clergy, i.e., those students now enrolled at two Southern Baptist seminaries.

In Hadden's (1967) study of 7,441 Protestant clergy, he found that among such denominations as the American Baptist and American Lutheran, the degree of consensus--when controlling for denomination--was low. For the American Baptist clergy, only 67 percent reached agreement on any one question. On two of the questions--those concerning the literal interpretation of the scripture, and the belief in the actual existence of Adam and Eve--no more than 55 percent of the Baptist clergy were in agreement. Similar disagreement also appears among Baptist clergy when the traditional doctrine of the church is brought into question. When the mission of the church in the secular world, and the social sources of ecumenicism were considered, however, substantial agreement did become apparent among the clergy in Hadden's study.

On the basis of this interdenominational study of the clergy, Hadden concludes that the source of the ecumenical movement does not lie in matters of doctrinal unity but, rather, in a common understanding of the position of the church in contemporary society--a conclusion Glock and Stark had previously reached as a result of their study of the laity. While the study reported herein does not attempt to investigate the ecumenical movement, it is suggested that a similar social base for church unity might be found within denominations, such as the Baptists, that are in disagreement on matters of doctrine and scripture.

PROCEDURES

In order to investigate the question of denominational unity, 300 Likert type questionnaires were mailed to seminary students attending two Baptist seminaries located in the deep south. From each seminary, 150 students were chosen by random sampling procedures to receive the questionnaires. A total of 233 questionnaires were completed and returned, for a response rate of 78 percent. The items used in our questionnaire were similar in nature to those used earlier by Glock and Stark, and Hadden.

Comparing the degree of consensus on the questionnaires we received, with the degree of consensus reported by Hadden's (1967) American Baptist clergy, it is suggested that our student sample will tend to under, rather than over, emphasize any actual differences that do occur in the Baptist church as a whole.[1] Comparison with Hadden's sample of clergy on the dimensions of interpretation of the scripture and the acceptance of traditional doctrine yields the results found in Table 1.

TABLE 1

PER CENT AGREEING AND DISAGREEING WITH THE INTERPRETATION OF THE
SCRIPTURE AND THE TRADITIONAL DOCTRINE OF THE CHURCH

INTERPRETATION OF SCRIPTURE	STUDENTS			CLERGY		
	AGREE	DISAGREE	(D)*	AGREE	DISAGREE	(D)*
1. I believe in a literal or nearly literal interpretation of the Bible.	64	36	28	43	57	14
2. As far as I am concerned, Adam and Eve were individual historical persons.	63	37	27	45	55	10
3. The Scriptures are the inspired and inerrant Word of God, not only in matters of faith but also in historical, geographical, and other secular matters.	56	44	12	33	67	34
4. An understanding of the language of myth and symbol are as important for interpreting Biblical literature as history and archeology.	56	44	12	62	48	14

* The smaller the (D), or difference, the more split are the respondents into two distinct groups.

63

TABLE 1 (Continued)

TRADITIONAL DOCTRINE OF CHURCH	STUDENTS			CLERGY		
	AGREE	DISAGREE	(D)*	AGREE	DISAGREE	(D)*
5. I believe the virgin birth of Jesus was a biological miracle.	86	14	72	65	44	12
6. I accept Jesus' physical resurrection as an objective historical fact in the same sense that President John Kennedy's death was a historical fact.	91	9	82	67	33	34
7. I believe in a divine judgment after death where some shall be rewarded and others punished.	91	9	82	71	29	42
8. I believe in the demonic as a personal power in the world.	84	16	68	67	33	34
9. Man, by himself, is incapable of anything but sin.	68	32	36	40	60	20

* The smaller the (D), or difference, the more split are the respondents into two distinct groups.

A discrepancy value was computed for both the students and clergy by taking the absolute value of the difference between the percent of respondents agreeing with each statement, and the percent of respondents disagreeing with each statement. As this absolute value grows smaller, the number of respondents agreeing and the number of respondents disagreeing with each statement approaches equality. The smaller this absolute value, the greater is the amount of disagreement expressed among members of the sample on each statement.

Table 1 indicates that the discrepancy value computed for the students is greater than that computed for the clergy on all but two statements (statements three and four). On these two statements, the difference between the value for the students and that for the clergy is quite small. The higher values for the students suggest that they are in greater agreement than are the clergy concerning the question of the traditional interpretation of the scripture and the traditional doctrine of the church. The greater consensus would tend to indicate that any differences found among the student sample would actually understate the disagreement, if any, that exists among the Baptist clergy. The higher student values may be due in part to the active learning role the students assume while in the seminary-- a role that would stress the church's traditional stand on matters of doctrine.

Theological and Ideological Position of the Students

An analysis of the responses given by the students shows that they are divided on most questions concerning the interpretation of the scriptures. These data are presented in Table 2. The question regarding the use of myth and symbol in interpreting the scripture showed the greatest amount of agreement among the student respondents (76 percent of the replies agreed with this statement). Less division was shown on the questions regarding the traditional doctrine of the church (it was on this dimension that the clergy sampled by Hadden (1967) were most widely split). The statement concerning the belief in Original Sin (question 9) was the subject of most disagreement between the students--68 percent professed belief in man's sinful nature and 32 percent did not.

Statements about the degree of tolerance of doubt and ambiguity in matters of belief split the respondents on two out of the three questions. The first statement, "Ambiguity and uncertainty as to what one is to believe and do are signs

65

TABLE 2

PERCENT AGREEING WITH INTERPRETATION OF SCRIPTURE, TRADITIONAL DOCTRINE, TOLERANCE OF DOUBT
AMBIGUITY, MISSION OF THE CHURCH, AND SOCIAL SOURCES OF ECUMENICISM

		PERCENT	N
1.	I believe in a literal or nearly literal interpretation of the Bible.	64	149
2.	As far as I am concerned, Adam and Eve were individual historical persons.	63	146
3.	The scriptures are inspired and inerrant Word of God, not only in matters of faith but also in historical, geographical and other secular matters.	56	130
4.	An understanding of the language of myth and symbol are as important for interpreting the Biblical literature as history and archeology.	76	178
5.	I believe that the virgin birth of Jesus was a biological miracle.	86	201
6.	I accept Jesus' physical resurrection as an objective historical fact in the same sense that President John Kennedy's death was a historical fact.	91	212
7.	I believe in a divine judgment after death where some shall be rewarded and others punished.	91	212
8.	I believe in the demonic as a personal power in the world.	84	197
9.	Man by himself is incapable of anything but sin.	68	159
10.	Ambiguity and uncertainty as to what one is to believe and do are signs of faithlessness and indifference to God.	15	35
11.	I would expect a thinking Christian to have doubts about the existence of God.	46	107

TABLE 2 (Continued)

	PERCENT	N
12. I have greater admiration for an honest agnostic seeking truth than a Christian who is certain he has the complete truth.	46	108
13. For the most part, the churches have been woefully inadequate in facing up to the civil rights issues.	82	190
14. Many whites pretend to be very Christian while in reality their attitudes demonstrate their lack of or misunderstanding of Christianity.	89	207
15. Christian education needs to bring laymen face-to-face with urban problems and propose solutions.	80	187
16. The churches should initiate inquiries into the implications of Christian convictions for the relations of the sexes, not assuming that there is any actual consensus in the churches on sexual morality.	75	175
17. The Christian is confined to no single method of gaining knowledge, but can make use of a plurality of methods relevant to the judgment to be made or the question under study.	90	209
18. The Christian church can only be its true self as it exists for humanity.	61	142
19. The primary task of the church is to live the Christian life among its own membership and activities rather than try and reform the world.	8	18

TABLE 2 (Continued)

	PERCENT	N
20. The church must speak to the great social issues of our day, or else its very existence is threatened.	73	170
21. The church should be taking a much more active role in the struggle for world peace.	66	155

Interpretation of Scripture: items 1-4.
Traditional Doctrine of Church: items 5-9.
Tolerance of Doubt and Ambiguity: items 10-12.
Social Sources of Ecumenicism: items 13-17.
Mission of the Church: items 18-21.

68

of faithlessness and indifference to God," drew the greatest consensus from the student sample. Eighty-five percent disagreed with this statement. The remaining statements split the sample into two rather distinct groups, 46 percent agreeing, and 54 percent disagreeing.

Students Position on the Secular Mission of the Church

The question of the mission of the church in the secular world also split the students, but to a lesser degree. Nearly all of the students disagreed with the statement that the church should confine its activities to its own membership rather than try to reform the world. The statement that the Christian church can only be its true self as it exists for humanity was agreeable to slightly more than 60 percent of the students. Over two-thirds agreed with the statement that the church should take a more active role in the struggle for world peace. Three-quarters of the sample thought the continued existence of the church was dependent upon it being able to speak to the great social issues of the day. Overall, there was a greater degree of consensus exhibited by the students on this dimension than when considering either the interpretation of the scripture, or their tolerance of doubt and ambiguity.

The most uniform responses occurred when the social sources of the ecumenical movement were brought into question. On every statement, at least three-quarters of the sample were in agreement. Ninety per-cent thought that a Christian is confined to no single method of gaining knowledge but could make use of a plurality of relevant methods. Eighty-two percent thought that for the most part, churches have been woefully inadequate in facing up to the civil rights issue. A similar question, "Many whites pretend to be very Christian while in reality their attitudes demonstrate their lack of or misunderstanding of Christianity," indicated that 89 percent of the students agreed.

These responses suggest that there is a denominational schism among the Southern Baptist divinity students in this sample, especially in those areas that relate to the way the scripture is to be interpreted and to the degree of tolerance that is felt for expressions of doubt and ambiguity. The students in the sample seem more closely aligned, however, when questions of the doctrine of the church and the social sources of ecumenicism are formulated. But further analysis, controlling for religious self-definition, suggests that there

69

is also a wide split among the prospective clergy on the question of church doctrine.

Theological Position of Students: Religious Self-Definition Controlled.

In terms of religious self-definition, 68 percent of the students labeled themselves as religiously conservative, 24 percent as religiously moderate, and 9 percent defined themselves as religiously liberal.[2] As Table 3 illustrates, the overrepresentation of conservative students gave false indications of unity on several questions. When responses are again examined, controlling for religious self-definition, a split in denominational unity is apparent, especially of the dimension regarding the traditional doctrine of the church.

Controlling for religious self-definition, the responses given to questions dealing with the interpretation of the scriptures, indicates the three groups show little agreement. On the item "I believe in a literal or nearly literal interpretation of the Bible," 79 percent of the religiously conservative, 25 percent of the religiously moderate, and 20 percent of the religiously liberal students expressed agreement. On item two, 78 percent of the conservatives, 36 percent of the moderates, and 10 percent of the liberals agreed that as far as they were concerned, "Adam and Eve were individual historical persons." A similar division was apparent on statement three, "The scriptures are the inspired and inerrant Word of God not only in matters of faith but also in historical, geographical and other secular matters. On this statement, 71 percent of the conservatives, 29 percent of the moderates, and 10 percent of the liberals agreed. Statement four, concerning the understanding of the language of myth and symbol in interpreting Biblical literature, had general approval (71 percent of the conservatives, 89 percent of the moderates, and 85 percent of the liberals agreed).

Without controlling for religious self-definition, the students appeared to show uniform agreement with the traditional doctrine of the church. Controlling for religious self-definitions shows this not to be the case. Ninety-four percent of the conservatives believed the virgin birth of Jesus to be a biological miracle (item 5). Seventy-six percent of the moderates also agreed with the statement, but only fifty percent of the liberal students held a similar view. While 99 percent of the conservatives agreed with

TABLE 3

PERCENT AGREEING WITH INTERPRETATION OF SCRIPTURE, TRADITIONAL DOCTRINE,
TOLERANCE OF DOUBT AND AMBIGUITY, MISSION OF THE CHURCH, SOCIAL
SOURCES OF ECUMENICISM: RELIGIOUS SELF-DEFINITION CONTROLLED

	Religious Self-Definition		
	(N=158) Conservative	(N=55) Moderate	(N=20) Liberal
1. I believe in a literal or nearly literal interpretation of the Bible.	79 (126)	25 (19)	20 (4)
2. As far as I am concerned, Adam and Eve were individual historical persons.	78 (124)	36 (20)	10 (2)
3. The scriptures are inspired and inerrant Word of God, not only in matters of faith but also in historical, geographical, and other secular matters.	71 (112)	29 (16)	10 (2)
4. An understanding of the language of myth and symbol are as important for interpreting the biblical literature as history and archeology.	71 (112)	89 (49)	85 (17)
5. I believe that the virgin birth of Jesus was a biological miracle.	94 (149)	76 (42)	50 (10)
6. I accept Jesus' physical resurrection as an objective historical fact in the same sense that President John Kennedy's death was a historical fact.	94 (149)	89 (49)	70 (14)

71

TABLE 3 (Continued)

| | Religious Self-Definition | | |
	(N=158) Conservative	(N=55) Moderate	(N=20) Liberal
7. I believe in a divine judgment after death where some shall be rewarded and others punished.	99 (151)	91 (50)	50 (10)
8. I believe in the demonic as a personal power in the world.	92 (146)	75 (41)	50 (10)
9. Man by himself is incapable of anything but sin.	73 (116)	66 (36)	35 (7)
10. Ambiguity and uncertainty as to what one is to believe and do are signs of faithlessness and indifference to God.	18 (28)	9 (5)	10 (2)
11. I would expect a thinking Christian to have doubts about the existence of God.	35 (56)	62 (34)	85 (17)
12. I have greater admiration for an honest agnostic seeking truth than a Christian who is certain he has the complete truth.	39 (62)	55 (30)	80 (16)
13. For the most part, the churches have been woefully inadequate in facing up to the civil rights issues.	76 (121)	89 (49)	100 (20)

TABLE 3 (Continued)

	Religious Self-Definition		
	(N=158) Conservative	(N=55) Moderate	(N=20) Liberal
14. Many whites pretend to be very Christian while in reality their attitudes demonstrate their lack of or misunderstanding of Christianity.	85 (135)	96 (53)	95 (19)
15. Christian education needs to bring laymen face-to-face with urban problems and propose solutions.	74 (118)	93 (51)	90 (18)
16. The churches should initiate inquiries into the implications of Christian convictions for the relations of the sexes, not assuming that there is any actual consensus in the churches on sexual morality.	62 (99)	76 (42)	75 (15)
17. The Christian is confined to no single method of gaining knowledge, but can make use of a plurality of methods relevant to the judgment to be made or the question under study.	87 (138)	93 (51)	100 (20)
18. The Christian church can only be its true self as it exists for humanity.	55 (88)	69 (38)	80 (16)
19. The primary task of the church is to live the Christian life among its own membership and activities rather than try and reform the world.	9 (14)	5 (3)	5 (1)

TABLE 3 (Continued)

| | Religious Self-Definition | | |
	(N=158) Conservative	(N=55) Moderate	(N=20) Liberal
20. The church must speak to the great social issues of our day, or else its very existence is threatened.	66 (105)	86 (47)	90 (18)
21. The church should be taking a much more active role in the struggle for world peace.	60 (95)	76 (42)	90 (18)

Interpretation of scripture: items 1-4
Traditional Doctrine of Church: items 5-9
Tolerance of Doubt and Ambiguity: items 10-12
Social Sources of Ecumenicism: items 13-17
Mission of the Church: items 18-21

74

item seven--"I believe in a divine judgment after death"--
91 percent of the moderates and only 50 percent of the
liberals held the same view. A belief in the demonic as an
existing personal power in the world (item 8) was expressed
by 92 percent of the conservative and 75 percent of the
moderate students. Again, only 50 percent of the liberals
in the sample agreed with the statement. Item 9, "Man by
himself is incapable of anything but sin," appealed to 73
percent of the conservatives, 66 percent of the moderates,
and 35 percent of the liberals. Only on the questions of
the physical resurrection of Jesus, was any large amount of
agreement shared by the students. Ninety-four percent of
the conservatives, 89 percent of the moderates and 70 percent of the liberals agreed with the statement concerning
the resurrection of Jesus (item 6).

While the majority of liberals agreed with statements
showing a tolerance of doubt and ambiguity in Christian
belief, most conservatives disagreed with the same statements. The moderates were about equally split on this
dimension with slightly more than half answering in a conservative manner.

Students Position on the Secular Mission of the Church: Religious Self-Definition Controlled

Concerning the mission of the church, more than fifty
percent of the conservatives believed that the church should
take a more active role in secular life, concern itself with
problems of world peace, and speak to the great social issues
of our time. Approximately 70 percent of the moderates and
over 80 percent of the liberals also thought the mission of
the church should involve itself more in the secular world.
The liberals voiced the strongest opinion of this nature.
Ninety percent agreed, both with the statement, "The church
must speak to the great social issues of our day or else its
very existence is threatened," and with the statement, "The
church should take a more active role in the struggle for
world peace." All three groups strongly disagreed with the
belief that the church should concern itself with living a
Christian life only among its own members rather than to try
to reform the world. Nine percent of the conservatives and
only five percent among the moderates and the liberals could
agree with this role for the Southern Baptist church.

The social sources of ecumenicism provide the basis for
the most uniformity among all three groups. As would be

expected, the liberals exhibited the strongest agreement on these statements. Two of the statements, that concerning the church's inadequacy in facing up to the civil rights issue (item 17), and that supporting the belief that a Christian can make use of a plurality of methods when seeking knowledge (item 21), were unanimously agreed upon by liberals. On item 17, 76 percent of the conservatives and 89 percent of the moderates agreed, while on item 21, 87 percent of the conservative students and 93 percent of the moderate students agreed. As regards the statement that although many whites pretend to be very Christian, in reality they demonstrate their lack of, or misunderstanding of, Christianity, all three groups were in general agreement.

It is evident that when the students are divided into three groups according to their religious self-definition, little consensus between the groups exists on questions concerning the interpretation of the scripture, the interpretation of traditional doctrine of the church, or the tolerance of doubt and ambiguity. More agreement exists on the interpretation of the mission of the church in the secular world. The greatest consensus is expressed on those statements concerning the social sources of ecumenicism.

Year of seminary training and age of the respondents did not add additional explanatory power as to the nature of these data. The data suggest (although not presented here) that except for a slight trend towards conservatism, the seminary does little to influence the doctrinal or scriptual views of its students.

SUMMARY

The purpose of this study was to investigate the possible sources of denominational unity. If there is a consensus of belief exhibited by the members of a denomination on questions concerning the interpretation of scripture, the traditional doctrine of the church, and the tolerance of doubt and ambiguity, then the basis for denominational unity may well be founded in a concern over sacred matters. But, if the members of the denomination do not show consensus in these areas, then we must look elsewhere for the forces that tend to unify the denomination.

Analysis of responses received from 233 divinity students at two Southern Baptist seminaries, indicates that the students may find little to agree upon when the scripture, doctrine, and tolerance of the church is brought into question. When control for religious self-definition is introduced into the study, the students are split into three distinct groups whose beliefs on these sacred matters show little similarity.

However, when the students are questioned about the mission of the church in the secular world and the social sources of ecumenicism, they show much greater consensus. Even when controlling for religious self-definition, little difference appears in the percentages of each group agreeing with statements of the church's secular role.

Controlling for the additional factors of age and year of seminary training, yields little additional information. There is a slight trend towards a more conservative religious attitude exhibited by those who are older and by those who are more advanced in their seminary training. Neither of these trends appear to be significant.

Religious self-definition appears to be a useful and accurate predictor of responses to other questions. Those individuals who identify themselves as conservative usually responded in a conservative manner on other statements. The same is true of liberals, and moderate responses were usually equally distributed among conservative and liberal responses to statements.

The concern for the position of the church in contemporary society: the agreement on the role the church should play in the secular world; and the social sources of ecumenicism might well be the foundation for the continued existence of contemporary Southern Baptist denominations. The students in this sample seem to overlook the differences of opinion that they hold on sacred matters, and find common identity in their concern for the future of the church and its position in the secular world.

FOOTNOTES AND REFERENCES

* We gratefully acknowledge the support made available for this project by the Auburn University Grant-in-Aid fund, Auburn University, Auburn, Alabama.

1. The comparison of American Baptist clergy and Southern Baptist Seminary students is presented for illustrative purposes only. The authors are aware of the differing theological and doctrinal positions the two faiths occupy. The results are intended, therefore, as suggestive.

2. Religious Self-Definition was obtained by asking the students to respond to the question: "With respect to religion do you consider yourself to be." The possible alternatives were very conservative, fairly conservative, moderate, fairly liberal, very liberal. In this paper the categories are collapsed to conservative, liberal, and moderate.

Glock, Charles Y., and Rodney Stark
  1965 Is There an American Protestantism? Trans-action, November/December, 13-18, 48-49.

Hadden, Jeffrey K.
  1967 A Protestant Paradox--Divided They Merge. Trans-action, July/August, 63-69.

PART THREE

RELIGIOSITY AND SEX

MALES, FEMALES AND RELIGION

Glenn M. Vernon and Jerry D. Cardwell*

There is a widely accepted belief that generally females are more religious than males. There are research findings which support this common sense observation. Little direct attention, however, has been given to these differences. There appears to be no article devoted exclusively to this subject.

The differences between the behavior of males and females in general is most likely one of which individuals have always been aware, and is probably one of the first ones of which an individual becomes aware in any society since many socio-cultural factors call attention thereto. This difference is likewise one of the most persistent differences. When behavioral scientists began to do research, it is likely that the male-female difference was one of the first ones explored. The researcher today who does not make a male-female distinction is likely to be asked why he didn't. It is somewhat surprising, then, that greater attention has not been given to male-female differences in religion.

While research in the sociology of religion has taken

male-female differences into account, little effort has been made to identify exceptions to the generalization that females tend to be more religious than males, or to explore the question of whether female religiosity is different from male religiosity. When attention is called to this area in the literature it is usually limited in scope and frequently not well documented. In an effort to remedy this situation somewhat, this paper analyzes the limited findings from various research efforts seeking to identify patterns which distinguish males and females. Our basic goal here is to provide a compilation of what has been found. This resource may then be used as a foundation from which explorations of the meaning of such differences can be given greater attention.

The identified differences, although being the behavior of individuals who are biologically different, do not stem directly from these biological differences per se. The behavioral differences are in part a result of different learning experiences, which incorporate socially constructed plans of actions which call for different types of male and female behavior. Emergent or non-scripted behavior is also no doubt involved. As social scientific interpretations of behavior have moved from biological determinism to interactionism, we have become increasingly aware of the importance of distinguishing between (1) any biological differences per se and (2) what is done about these differences. Behavior which takes biological differences into account is socially constructed phenomenon, and is symbolic in nature. The identified male-female difference then stems from expectations, obligations, and emergent definitions associated with human sexual differences. These are socially constructed.

Awareness of definitions and behavioral differences is acquired in informal as well as formal (research) ways. The knowledge of a society includes beliefs about such differences secured through many different methods including common sense. In some cases the formal research supports, in others qualifies, and in others contradicts the common sense meanings.

Male-female differences will be explored in the areas of religiosity, attendance, membership and leadership, clergymen and clergywomen, and family, marriage and sexual characteristics.

Religiosity

Religiosity is a widely-used but difficult concept to

define and is consequently a difficult concept to research. What frequently happens is that one or two factors such as church attendance and belief in God are accepted as indicators of what is conceived of as the more inclusive concept "religiosity." However, recently more sophistication has been introduced, with the concept of religiosity being subdivided into various dimensions. Examination is being made of the relationships between these dimensions. Most of the research surveyed here is of the unidimensional type. There may be an advantage at this stage of development of the field, in eliminating the "religiosity concept" and working with individual elements or combinations of elements without assuming that each is somehow related to the broader "religiosity" concept. At least the relative influence of the various components could be studied, as Cardwell has done. The relationship between various elements can be explored. Such exploration might lead to the development of new concepts which in turn might prove to be more useful than the broad religiosity concept. To date, there has been little in the way of consistent research findings as regards the multidimensional concept of religiosity. The number of possible dimensions has varied, based on reported research, from five to more than twenty.

The majority of research available does not evidence a consistent definition of religiosity. Consequently, the various reported research findings are not necessarily taking into account exactly the same thing. We will assume that there is sufficient harmony between them, however, to justify including them in the same section of the paper and to justify reaching some tentative conclusions about the religiosity of males and females.

Our analysis of the differences identified in the research will in part utilize concepts not utilized in the research, but which appear to be of utility in a sociological analysis of religious behavior. We distinguish among church religion, individual or unaffiliated religion, societal religion, and cosmis or universal religion.

Religion per se is conceptualized as involving definitions of the supernatural and/or high intensity value-moral definitions, and behavior which takes these definitions into account.

Church religion or church-type religion consists of such definitions and behavior which involve a formally organized, church group. A major raison d'etre for the group is the

81

perpetuation and application of the religious beliefs. It is recognized by those familiar with the group that it is related to religion.

Societal religion consists of the configuration of definitions of the supernatural and/or high intensity value definitions which serve to integrate a particular society. Such religion is frequently identified as the mores or the primary value structure of a society. When sociologists or anthropologists talk about the integrative function of religion it is usually societal religion (not church religion) to which they refer. It is likely that most readers of such writings interpret them as saying that church religion serves this integrating function. Such a conclusion is usually not accurate. When there is one established church for one society, church religion and societal religion somewhat coincide. However, to the extent that the church and the state are identified as separate institutions, societal religion may have dimensions not included in church religion and church religion incorporates dimensions such as group maintenance, which are not a part of societal religion. In the U.S. where there are many churches within one society, distinct differences obtain between church religion and societal religion. Societal religion has been called civil religion by Bellah, American religion by Herberg, and the Invisible religion by Luckmann.

Cosmic religion involves definitions of the supernatural and high intensity value defintions which are involved in definitions and experiences which are believed to transcend societal boundaries. These are the definitions which are brought into play when the individual or the group thinks in the most expansive manner of which each is capable. Such religion involves definitions about all of humanity, of all of mankind. Such definitions usually include not only the living, but individuals from the past and the future as well. Being a symbol user, man can make either or both the past and the future symbolically present and take such definitions into account. When decisions are reached about how beings everywhere should behave, or about how the supernatural (god, the gods, or whatever non-human aspects are taken into account) relates to human beings everywhere, such behavior is incorporated within the category of cosmic religion. As the experienced space of the world has decreased in size, it is likely that the extent of value consensus shared by all groups has increased. Most likely no one can with any degree of accuracy specify the beliefs involved and the extent of agreement with reference thereto. However, it would seem safe to hypothesize that movement in the direction of the establishment of a cosmic religion is taking place.

Independent-unaffiliated religion is found at the indivi- dual level and includes religious definitions and behavior which are meaningful to the individual but which are not necessarily incorporated in a church-group structure, even though the beliefs may be somewhat identical with those endorsed by church members or groups. Even if the content is identical, the "package" in which it is contained is none- theless different. Different packaging may result in different related behavior.

Obviously there is overlap between these four categories. Each, however, is an identifiable phenomenon. Individual members of church groups or the church as a group may, of course, believe or define their religious beliefs as being cosmic in nature or as applying to everyone everywhere. The Catholic conception of natural law approximates this concept. However, the value consensus which helps to integrate a society may involve aspects not included in any particular church religion.

A particular individual may be committed to beliefs incor- porated in both church religion and societal religion. He may, of course, have beliefs not so included. In any event, the fact that his beliefs are not emmeshed in a larger church- religion configuration or a larger societal-religion configu- ration gives them a distinctive characteristic. It is our belief, however, that utilization of these categories will provide more meaningful understanding of man's religious be- havior than use of the one all-inclusive concept of religion.

Clearly it is to church religion that most of the research and theorizing has been related up to date. This is probably a result of the fact that indicants of church religion are more easily identified and operationalized.

In the research included in Table I, religiosity has been measured in many different ways. Included here is research which specifically described that which was measured as "religiosity." Research dealing specifically with church attendance is presented in Table II. As has been suggested, the utility of such an undefined broad category is somewhat questionable. There is some overlap between categories used here and those included in subsequent sections. Details on

83

Table I

RELIGIOSITY

Researcher	Universe of Study	Variables Used in Comparisons		
		Female Higher	Male Higher	Male-Female Similarity
Anderson	Young unmarried - Tompkin County NY	Membership		
Argyle	Various - U.S. & English, Christians	Religiosity (prayer-member, attendance, etc.)		
	Jewish		Religiosity	
Abramson	U.S. Catholic Ethnic Groups	Religiosity		
Bain	U.S. Students	Conservative Beliefs	Liberal Beliefs	Belief in God and Immortality
Bardis	Jewish Students			Religiosity
Bemporad	Jewish children in treatment center for emotional disturbance	Problem with religious identity		
Blood & Wolfe	Michigan	Religiosity		

Researcher	Universe of Study	Variables Used in Comparisons		
		Female Higher	Male Higher	Male-Female Similarity
Brookover et al.	Michigan State Students	Increasing in religiosity in college		Lowering of commitment to beliefs and specific group in college
Carlson	U. of Chicago Students	Belief in God		
Cline and Richards	Mormons	Belief, convictions, activity conform to beliefs, "know" religion		
Didate and Kennedy	Students	Religious values		
Kynes	U.S.	Religious interest		
Dempsey and Pandey	Australia	Beliefs and practices		
Erskine	U.S. polls	Read entire Bible Value sabbath		
	Poll data	Belief in God, that Jesus will return, & in life after death		

Researcher	Universe of Study	Variables Used in Comparisons		
		Female Higher	Male Higher	Male-Female Similarity
Frerking	U.S.	Cultic, Credal Devotional	Cognitive	
Fukuyama	Congregational Church	Cultic, Credal Devotional	Cognitive	
Gaffin 1952 & Gallup Poll 1967	Poll data	Concern with life after death		
Gans	Boston's West End	Church identification, ritualistic	Religious Id. contrasted with church Id.	
Garrison	Students	Church minded		
Gilliland	Students			Religious attitudes
Glenn	Poll data	Have definite opinions on religion		
Gorer	England	Prayers		
Gorer	England - bereaved individuals	Belief in blissful after life		

Researcher	Universe of Study	Variables Used in Comparisons		
		Female Higher	Male Higher	Male-Female Similarity
Hammond	Congregational Christian Church	Conservative Beliefs	Like to argue about religion and doubt religious beliefs as science training increases	
Hardy	Mormon			Favorable to religion
Hiemstra	Normal & psychiatric patients	Choice of most & least preferred biblical character		
Hutchinson	U.S.	Defined as active by clergy		
Jones	Students	Conservative morality		
Kryvelev	USSR	Reject atheism Accept traditional religion	Accept atheism	
Lenski	U.S.	Religious interest		
Lindenfeld	Upwardly mobile, U.S.		Importance of religion	

Researcher	Universe of Study	Variables Used in Comparisons		
		Female Higher	Male Higher	Male-Female Similarity
London, et al.	Students	Religious doctrine		
Main	U.S. - only church attenders			Religiosity
Moreton	England	Attendance		Favorable to religion
Mulford & Salisbury	Iowa	Religion Id. on TST		
Nash & Berger	Congregational	Church activities		
O'Reilly	Older people	Activity		
Putney & Snell	Students	Orthodoxy, value religious self-definitions		Missionary zeal

any particular research can, of course, be secured by consulting the original source.

Very clearly the over-all pattern on religiosity shown in Table I, is one of higher female than male religiosity on the majority of the variables included. Attendance, considered as a separate item in Table II, is sometimes included as the findings with reference to attendance support those concerning religiosity. The research included in Table II indicates that on the whole, when just church attendance is considered, women tend to attend more regularly and more frequently than do men. Some surveys show a trend toward equal attendance, but no research except some dealing with Jewish and Mormon attendance, indicates that men attend more frequently than females. Catholic men attend more frequently than Protestant men (see Fichter).

These same exceptions are found with reference to religiosity. The exceptions are the Jews (Argyle, Bardis, Bemporad, Lazerwitz) and the Mormons (Cline and Richards, Hardy, Vernon). This limited evidence is, of course, far from conclusive, but it does suggest that in these two groups the pattern of higher female religiosity and attendance does not obtain. Rather, there is either higher or equal male religiosity.

The distinctive patterns of male involvement for the Jews and the Mormons may be related to the fact that each of these church groups and their religious activities are male oriented. The role definitions of the church organization incorporate patterns of male superioity and female subordination. Individual, societal, and cosmic religion may include such super-subordination beliefs. Church religion, however, reinforces the beliefs with organization, bureaucratic interaction in which such beliefs are given behavioral expression. This increases the likelihood of male superiority and the likelihood that males will exceed females in their religious behavior.

In the Mormon church, the priesthood is an exclusive male phenomenon. Females are given important roles to play in auxiliary organizations, but such roles and their organizations are clearly defined as auxiliary and therefore of a different nature than the essential male organization. There is no female clergy. Among the Jews a similar pattern obtains, and it is only within recent months that a female cantor has emerged.

In church religion where the role definitions specify high male involvement, such involvement is higher than otherwise.

Table II

CHURCH ATTENDANCE

Researcher	Universe of Study	Female High	Male High	Same
Abramson	Catholic ethnic gps.*; Ethnic endogamy**	* X		** X
Bourland 1960	Rural France	X		
DeWitt	Canada (Lutheran)	X		
Eister 1952	Students, Southern Methodists	X		
Fichter	Catholics - Mass attendance	X		
	Communion, confession & Lenten & evening services			X
Fogarty	West Germany	X		
Gorer	England - Bereaved	X		
Hadden & Evans	Students	X		
Lazerwitz 1962	U.S. surveys - Christian	X		
	Jewish		X	
Remmers & Radler	U.S.	X		
Schuyler	Catholics - U.S.	X		
	Europe	X		
	Latin America	X		
Van Houtte	Western Europe	X		

90

The research by Frerking and that by Fukuyama supports the premise that male religiosity and female religiosity may be somewhat different. Each researcher found that when the broad "religiosity" concept is broken down into four component parts, the males may exceed the females on knowledge about religion (the cognitive dimension), while the females exceed the males on the other three dimensions--i.e., cultic, credal and devotional. If this is a somewhat general pattern, most other less sophisticated research apparently covers up this difference.

There may be a relationship between this high knowledge-orientation and the fact that Hammond found that males more than females like to argue about religion, and that they are more inclined to doubt religion as their training in science increases. It may be that they know more to argue about. Knowledge about something is quite different from commitment thereto. Schofield's findings that males more than females endorse the premise that the good life need not include religion is also relevant, if the respondents interpreted "religion" here to mean "church religion."

Gans' findings are also suggestive. The fact that the West End Bostonian males identify more with religion than the church, whereas, the females identify more with the church than with religion, suggests a broader male perspective. Males may be more concerned than females with unaffiliated or maybe nonaffiliated religion (skipping church religion) and with societal or maybe cosmic religion. Limited loyalty to a specific church group is also suggested by Taggart's finding that males more than females approve of ecumenism.

Russian males are more accepting of state endorsed atheism than are Russian females. This suggests again the greater male concern with societal religion and less concern with church religion.

Male endorsement of societal religion is also suggested by Main's study which was restricted to church attenders. When only church attenders are considered, he found about equal male and female religiosity. However, attenders included a higher percent of females than males. This may be related to the Mormon and Jewish patterns just discussed. In both of these groups there are strong organizational expectations that males will attend and participate. This higher participation of males is related to higher religiosity.

For those Main studied expectations to participate and related actual participation would then be greater for males who attend than for males who do not attend. It would be surprising then if this did not lead to higher religiosity of attending males than nonattending males.

Strong taboos against female participation and very limited actual participation are found in Islam.

The distinctive female religiosity characteristics may be related to the fact that females have been found to be more willing than males to disclose details about themselves to others. Research by Hood and Back, Jourard, and DeBeauvoir indicate that women disclose their personal feelings to each other with greater frequency than men do. In the Jourard study, males rated a competition experiment highest whereas females rated an affiliation experiment highest.

Lowenthal and Haven (p. 30) also emphasize this female characteristic and suggest another possible consequence thereof.

> At this stage of our knowledge, we can only wonder whether women's greater sensitivity to close relationships, as their greater versatility in the choice of objects for such relationships, has any causal connection with their greater adaptability for survival. Not only is the overall death rate higher among men, but among them, and not among women, the suicide rate increases rapidly with age. And despite their greater potentiality for remarriage, it is among men not women that widowhood is more likely to trigger menatl illness . . . . Maintenance of closeness with another is the center of existence up to the very end of life.

Moberg (p. 399) explains the high female participation patterns as follows:

> Culture standards demand that women be more pious. Our institutional norms are different for women than for men. The family and 'culture-bearer' roles of women appear more consistent with the values and functions of religion than with the secular roles of the males.

The low male participation for St. Matthew's Lutheran Church in Canada was explained by one immigrant male member as typically being due to the fact that

92

. . . St. Matthew's is more set up for women anyway. They have the Women's Club and teas and so on, but I know that I don't have time for such things. . . . It's good for the women to take the children to church and the other things; every kid should have a religious upbringing. . . . I think the reason we (immigrant males) don't attend church too often is because we are too busy making a living. I try to get to Communion as often as possible, but I also have to work a lot on Sundays. . . .

Gans suggests that for the males from the West End of Boston, the attitude toward the church is based in large part on a lack of respect for the priesthood. For while priests are expected to be morally superhuman they are suspect for being not quite human enough--celibacy. The men have considerable regard for nuns who teach parochial school.

Lang suggests that the church's traditional "extra" activities as well as worship services may be more appropriate for females than males. The roles of women are chiefly family-centered, with a tendency to depend largely upon personal influences. Religion, dealing largely with personality, is perhaps more easily appreciated by them than by men.

Salisbury indicates that "the sex role differentiation data of his study support those other studies which have found that women tend to select interaction roles with a social-emotional rather than a task emphasis."

Krebs found that teachers tend to rate girls as more moral than boys on the three scales he used. These judgments, however, seem to have no basis in fact. On the "Moral Inventory Test" the girls did not make more "moral" judgments than the boys. In the middle-class group, the boys were more moral than the girls. In the cheating tests, there were no significant differences.

Krebs provides possible explanations as follows. Girls conform more than boys, and teachers may confuse conformity with morality. Girls are more eager to please, and teachers may see this eagerness as a sign of morality. Boys of the age treated have a less positive self-image than girls. These boys don't think very well of themselves, and it may be that their teachers react to the way the boys feel about themselves and not to their actual behavior.

The reactions of the teachers might reflect somewhat at least societal religion definitions about male-female

93

differences.

   Mormon patterns. Cline and Richards provide an analysis
of male-female differences for the Mormons they studied which
suggests greater similarity with the other religious groups
than has been so far indicated. The distinctive Mormon patterns are coupled with some rather common male-female differences. Their universe of study was 155 adult males and females from Salt Lake City. They concluded that for the female in their study the deeper and the more intense her religious beliefs and convictions were, the more likely she was
to behave and do things in her everyday life consistent with
these beliefs. Likewise, the more she participates behaviorally in religious activities, the greater the likelihood
that her belief and convictions will be strengthened. Males
were characterized by intense activity (high attendance,
hold church jobs, frequent prayer, etc.) but for the men more
than the females there was a greater degree of doubt, and
ambiguity in their beliefs about the nature of God, the
validity and accuracy of the scriptures, immortality, etc.
For men, it was found that some were very high in their religious activity yet at the same time came close to "failing"
a belief test. Contrariwise, some men were relatively inactive (in church religion) yet in terms of beliefs were deeply
religious (at the individual level). They had a deeply committed belief in the existence of God, in a life after death
and/or in the validity and accuracy of the scriptures, etc.
The males make more of a distinction between belief and
behavior than do females.

   They also found evidence that for some of the males
studied there was a tendency to become "unconverted" or to
reject the religion learned in youth. This involved a tendency to view church religion from a "theoretical or philosophical point of view" rather than to accept it by faith.
This coincided with doubt, conflict, considerable guilt and
an increasing rejection of a "literal interpretation" of the
scriptures. Finally there is a pragmatic demand for tangible
absolute proof for the religionists' claims, which when not
met leads to further estrangement and loss of faith but not
without some personal turmoil.

   It would be improper for a scientist to conclude that
males and females should be the same. If religion does function to relieve anxiety, insecurity, etc., then to the extent
that anxiety-insecurity differs from males to females, the
religious variables would be expected to evidence variability.

To the extent that male and female roles vary, they may each require distinctive types of validation, legitimation, etc.

To the extent that religion is the opiate of the people, different types of experiences and illnesses may require different types of "prescriptions" or tranquilizers.

To the extent that one sex attempts to dominate the others in the power structure, religion can be used in such efforts.

There may be differences in experiences of guilt, which again would be related to differences in efforts to do something about such guilt experiences.

Membership and Leadership

The available research findings clearly indicate that more women than men belong to churches. Ketch's study of 42,691 citizens of Springfield, Missouri, found 90.1 men per 100 female church members. Jordan found that in 19 churches of a small Oregon town most church members were women. Main's study of over 10,000 church attenders from 49 churches in Illinois found more male than female leaders. Hepple found in his Missouri study that females comprised 49% of the rural population but 55% of the participating church members. Lazerwitz (1964) found that slightly more Protestant men than women belong to voluntary associations of which the church is one, while Catholic men are clearly more active in voluntary associations than Catholic women. England studied letters of testimony written by Christian Science members and concluded (1) the largest single group from which the adherents of Christian Science are drawn are urban, middle-class, married females who are suffering from bodily disorders of physical or emotional origin, and (2) the tendency to become associated with this religion because of specific troubles is more characteristic of women than of men.

Lazerwitz's (1961) survey data reports relatively high female composition of Negro Baptists and Episcopalians. "Nones" (religious independents) were heavily male (81%).

The U.S. Census report on the Civilian Population of the United States 1956, shows that more women than men were reported as members of the major religious groups (Roucek). T. Lynn Smith summarized the results of the 1936 census of Religious Bodies. There was an over-all sex ratio of church

95

membership of 78.5 (78.5 males per 100 females). Religious bodies with the most children enrolled as members tended to have the most equitable sex distributions. The highest sex ratio (99.1) was reported by the Mormon Church. The Church of Christ, Scientist, had the lowest sex ratio (31.3). Southern denominations had higher sex ratios than their northern counterparts. The sex ratio of rural farm communities is far higher than that of urban areas.

With reference to non-U.S. studies, Zetterberg's study of Swedish Mission Youth Clubs found 16 female members for every 10 male members. DeWitt's study of Lutherans in New Brunswick, indicated equal membership although female attendance was higher.

Despite the fact that females are overrepresented in church membership the tendency is for men to be church leaders. Jordan's study of 19 churches of a small Oregon town indicated that most church leaders were male. Schuyler indicates that in the U.S. Catholic female leadership is less common than in European and Latin American countries. Taves reports that there is a trend for females to take an increasingly active role in church activities and to hold more church offices than formerly.

As has been indicated, Salisbury reports that women tend to select interaction roles with a social-emotional rather than those with a task emphasis. Leadership roles tend to be task oriented.

Increasing female leadership may be related to the Salisbury finding that males and females are in virtual agreement on the degree to which the equalitarian authority pattern is desirable. Siegman, however, found that women have a greater tendency to see God in punishing and fear-inspiring terms.

Clark's study of 754 males and 1,420 females from the records of 60 institutions of learning and two Methodist Summer assemblies for young people identified the following types of conversion patterns:

Types of Conversion	1,420 females	736 males
Definite Crisis	2.5%	14.6%
Emotional Stimulus	26.5%	27.7%
Gradual	71.0%	57.7%

Female conversion was more likely than the male to be gradual, although the majority of both types are in this category. Crisis conversion more frequent for males than females.

Clergywomen and Clergymen

When females do play leadership roles, important male-female difference are found. The female clergywoman is usually a second-class clergy. Jones and Taylor indicated that only one-third of their sample of clergywomen was able to move directly into ministerial positions upon completion of education and certification. Two-thirds of these clergywomen found it necessary to enter other occupations until ministerial positions were available to them.

Bock summarizes census data as follows:

1. The role of clergy has traditionally been masculine plus "sacredly" masculine. A father figure has been used extensively. The American Association of Women Ministers was founded in 1919 "to promote equal ecclesiastical rights for women and to encourage young women to take up the work of the ministry." There is a membership of 250 who are licensed, ordained or authorized to preach.

2. From 1900 to 1960 there was an increase in number of clergywomen, from 3,405 to 4,695--38%. However, the male clergy increased 81%. Of total clergy, females comprise 3.9% to 2.3% with considerable fluctuation which is hard to explain.

3. There is a larger percentage of male than female black clergy.

4. Male clergy are relatively older than female, in any decade until 1960. Today there is a tendency for clergywomen to be older. There may be recruiting problems for younger females.

5. Female clergy have a lower educational level than white and black clergymen.

6. Female clergy are less likely than clergymen to be married and to be living with spouse. This may be due to age and racial composition. Clergywomen more likely work part time. This suggests one solution to conflict with family and career. The relatively high percentage of absent

spouses may result from another solution. High divorce hints at still another solution. Evidence of career-marital conflict is also suggested by a large amount of fluctuation in young, single clergywomen.

7. Clergywomen report lower salaries than clergymen. There is little evidence for increased professionalization of clergywomen, greater acceptance of women as clergy, more use of the clergy by women as an occupational outlet, or improvement of the composite "woman preacher." The data raises a question about applying the label "profession" to these females. In some characteristics (education attainment) they are more like the general labor force than like other professionals. Differences between male and female in age, education and marital status are quite conspicuous and these distinctions suggest that clergy roles are different for females than for males or are differentially experienced. Opportunities for females to act as clergy are more limited and these limitations at least suggest professional marginality.

8. Sect-type groups appear to approve of female clergy more than denomination type (church type). Black females probably have greater opportunity to serve as clergywomen than do whites. Blacks are more likely affiliated with a sect, which is in turn more likely to accept female clergy.

Marriage, Family and Sexual Behavior

Intermarriage. There is no research indicating clearly that either men or women are more likely to intermarry. Besanceney reports that the intermarriage rates for Catholic men and women are not significantly different. The intermarriage rate is only slightly higher for Catholic men.

Besanceney from a secondary analysis of survey data from the Detroit area, concluded that intermarriage rates for Catholic men is not significantly different from that of Catholic women. There was a slight but not statistically significant tendency for Catholic men to be partners in an interfaith marriage more than Catholic women. "Most earlier studies have shown higher rates of intermarriage for Catholic women than for Catholic men. The ratio has gone as high as seven to three in two studies and as low as five to four in two others. Only in rural parishes of one Canadian diocese were Catholic men found to have intermarried at a higher rate than Catholic women." He reports that most earlier studies have shown that Catholic women intermarry more often than Catholic men, with the ratio varying from 7:3 to 5:4.

98

Bemporad's statistical data for Jews shows that Jewish males intermarry more frequently than Jewish females, as do male children of these marriages.

Abramson's study of intermarriage in ethnic groups does not clearly indicate the effect of intermarriage for Catholics. Although the total attendance falls 8% for females who marry exogamously while it stays the same for males, the trends vary considerably among individual ethnic groups.

In Abramson's study, for the total group he found no differences between the endogamous and exogamous respondents of either sex. The breakdown by ethnicity, however, did find that the Irish and French-Canadian Catholics lose some degree of church activity when they marry out, and this is true for both sexes. Although the differences are appreciably greater for males than for females, the directions are the same. German and Polish Catholics show no change following out-marriage, and sex as well makes no difference for the religious involvement of these two groups. German and Polish men are seemingly as likely to attend weekly Mass as the women of these nationalities. For the women of Italian and Spanish-speaking backgrounds, marriage outside of their respective groups makes some difference in increased church attendance. For the men of these two groups, this pattern is not in evidence.

Adams and Mogey studied Nashville, Tennessee, Disciples of Christ congregations. They found that husbands are more influential than wives in deciding which church a religiously mixed marriage should choose.

Family Behavior. Burchinal in a study of 256 couples from rural and small towns of four midwestern states found that (1) for males, higher marital satisfaction was reported for church members than for non-church members. Differences for females were in the same direction but were not statistically significant. When members and nonmembers are compared, greater differences obtain for males than for females. Females tend to be more religious than males.

David's study of 160 Jews found that husbands and wives evidenced about the same patterns of familism and that for both groups the correlation between familism and religiosity was high and positive.

Dyer and Luckey in a study of the marital happiness of

522 married couples found that there was no relationship between church affiliation and any of the five personality variables measured. For females, however, there were significant differences.

Sexual Behavior and Attitudes. Cardwell found that among University of Maine students, the influence of religiosity upon sexual attitudes was greater for females than males, for whom amount of education was of greater influence than religion. Ryppel replicated Cardwell's research using a sample of college students from a midwestern university. Lindenfeld found that among his college students those of higher religiosity tended to be sexually more restrictive than those of lower religiosity. Females would, on the basis of other data, be overrepresented among the high-religiosity students.

Semenfink studied married respondents in Louisiana and northeastern U.S. Roman Catholic males were stronger than Roman Catholic females in their rejection of their church position on use of contraceptives. Similarly, a higher percent of Roman Catholic males than Roman Catholic females reported use of contraceptives before and after marriage.

Christensen and Carpenter found that liberal attitudes toward sexual behavior were higher for males than females in three widely divergent societies: Utah with its conservative predominantly Mormon sexual standards, Indiana which is approximately average for the U.S., and Denmark which typified the rather liberal sex codes of Scandinavia.

Summary

Research supports the common observation that generally females tend to be more religious than males. The generalization, however, is qualified by research including the finding that among the Jews and the Mormons, males appear to be equal to or greater than females on measures of religiosity and attendance. In general, leadership is predominantly male. There are also religiously related differences in marriage and sexual behavior. Male and female religious experiences appear to be different in both degree and kind. Understanding of differences is increased if a distinction is made among cosmic, societal, church and independent religion. Differences appear to be related to other social factors and have consequences for the behavior of those involved.

REFERENCES CITED

Abramson, Harold J.
   1966   "Inter-Ethnic Marriage Among American Catholics
          and Changes in Religious Behavior," paper presented
          at the meetings of the Society for the Scientific
          Study of Religion, Chicago, October.

Adams, Robert Lynn and John Mogey
   1967   "Marriage, Membership and Mobility in the Church
          and Sect," Sociological Analysis, (Marquette
          University, Milwaukee, Wisc.), 28, 4, Winter,
          205-214.

Anderson, W. A.
   1937   Rural Youth: Activities, Interests, and Problems,
          Bulletin 661, (January), Cornell University Agri-
          cultural Experiment Station, Ithaca, N.Y.

Argyle, Michael
   1959   Religious Behavior. Free Press: Glencoe, Illinois,
          pp. 71-79.

Bain, Read
   1927   "Religious Attitudes of College Students," American
          Journal of Sociology, Vol. 32, pp. 762-770.

Bardis, Panos D.
   1964   "Religiosity Among Jewish Students in a Metropolitan
          Community," Sociology and Social Research, Vol. 49,
          No. 1 (October), pp. 90-96.

Bellah, Robert N.
   1967   "Civil Religion in America." Daedalus, 96 (Winter),
          pp. 1-21.

Bemporad, Jack, Rabbi
   1966   "Some Effects of Intermarriage on Children," in
          Zurotsky, Jack J., ed. The Psychological Implica-
          tions of Intermarriage. New York: Supreme
          Printing Company, Inc.

Bescanceney, Paul H.
   1965   "Interfaith Marriages of Catholics in the Detroit
          Area," Sociological Analysis, Vol. 26 (Spring),
          pp. 38-44.

Blood, Robert O. and Donald M. Wolfe
　1960　Husbands and Wives, New York: MacMillan Co.,
　　　　 reprinted in Bell, Robert R., ed. Studies in Mar-
　　　　 riage and the Family, New York: Thomas Y. Crowell,
　　　　 1968.

Bock, E. Wilbur
　1967　"The Female Clergy: A Case of Professional
　　　　 Marginality," American Journal of Sociology,
　　　　 Vol. 72, No. 5 (March), pp. 531-539.

Boulard, F.
　1960　"The Map of Religious Practice in Rural France,
　　　　 The Present Position of Geographical Research,"
　　　　 in Religion, Culture and Society, Louis Schneider,
　　　　 editor, New York: John Wiley & Sons, Inc., 1964,
　　　　 pp. 385-389.

Brookover, William, et. al.
　1965　The College Student, New York: The Center for
　　　　 Applied Research in Education, Inc., p. 66.

Burchinal, L. G.
　1957　"Marital Satisfaction and Religious Behavior,"
　　　　 American Sociological Review, 22/3, pp. 306-310.

Cardwell, Jerry D.
　1969　"The Relationship Between Religious Commitment and
　　　　 Attitudes Toward Premarital Sexual Permissiveness:
　　　　 A 5-D Analysis," Sociological Analysis, Summer,
　　　　 30, 2, pp. 72-80.

Carlson, Hilding B.
　1934　"Attitudes of Undergraduate Students," Journal
　　　　 of Social Psychology, Vol. 5, pp. 202-212.

Christensen, Harold T. and George R. Carpenter
　1962　"Value-Behavior Discrepancies Regarding Premarital
　　　　 Coitus in Three Western Cultures," American
　　　　 Sociological Review, Vol. 27, No. 1, February,
　　　　 pp. 66-74.

Cline, Victor B. and James M. Richards, Jr.
　1965　"A Factor Analytic Study of Religious Belief and
　　　　 Behavior," Journal of Personality and Social
　　　　 Psychology, Vol. 1, No. 6, pp. 569-578.

DeBeauvoir, Simon
1961   The Second Sex, (translated and edited by H. M.
        Parshley), New York: Bantam Books, 1961.

Dempsey, K. C. and Jennifer Pandey
1967   "The Religious Practices of First Year College
        Students," Australian Journal of Social Issues,
        3, 1, Spring, Armidale, New South Wales,
        Australia, pp. 1-8.

DeWitt, Robert Lee
1965   The Lutheran Church in Fredericton, Master's
        Thesis, The University of New Brunswick.

Didato, S. V. and T. M. Kennedy
1956   "Masculinity-Feminity and Personal Values,"
        Psychological Reports, Vol. 2, p. 231.

Dyer, Dorothy Tunnel and Eleanor Braun Luckey
1961   "Religious Affiliation and Selected Personality
        Scores as They Relate to Marital Happiness of a
        Minnesota College Sample," Marriage and Family
        Living, 23/1, pp. 46-47.

Dynes, Russell R.
1959   "The Relation of Community Characteristics of
        Religious Organization and Behavior," in Community
        Structure and Analysis, ed. Marvin B. Sussman,
        New York: Thomas Y. Crowell, p. 265, from Main,
        1967.

Eister, A. W.
1952   "Some Aspects of Institutional Behavior with
        Reference to Churches," American Sociological
        Review, Vol. 17, February, pp. 64-69.

Erskine, Hazel G.
1965   "The Polls: Personal Religion," Public Opinion
        Quarterly, 29 (Spring), p. 145.

Fichter, Joseph H.
1954   Social Relations in the Urban Parish, University
        of Chicago, pp. 61, 91-93.

Fogarty, Michael P.
1957   "Religious Statistics," in Religion, Culture, and
        Society, Louis Schneider, editor. New York: John
        Wiley & Sons, Inc., 1964, pp. 393-399.

Frerking, Ken
    1965   "Religious Participation of Lutheran Students,"
            Review of Religious Research, Spring, Vol. 6,
            No. 3, pp. 153-162.

Fukuyama, Yoshio
    1961   "The Major Dimensions of Church Membership,"
            Review of Religious Research, Spring, Vol. 2,
            pp. 154-161.

Gaffin, Ben
    1967   1952 study by Ben Gaffin and Associates under the
            supervision of Dr. Gallup and the 1966 one by
            Dr. Gallup's Public Opinion Surveys. Reported in
            Catholic Digest, May.

Gans, Herbert J.
    1967   "The Urban Villagers" from Derek L. Phillips (ed.)
            Studies in American Society: II, Thomas Y. Crowell
            Company, pp. 180-221. Reprinted from The Urban
            Villagers by Herbert J. Gans, The Free Press of
            Glencoe, 1962.

Garrison, Karl C.
    1962   "The Relationship of Certain Variables to Church-
            Sect Typology Among College Students," The Journal
            of Social Psychology, 56: 29-32.

Gilliland, A. R.
    1940   "The Attitude of College Students Toward God and
            Church," Journal of Social Psychology, Vol. II,
            pp. 11-18.

Glenn, Norval D.
    1968   "Aging, Disengagement, and Opinionation," forth-
            coming in The Public Opinion Quarterly (Now in
            mimeographed form).

Gorer, Geoffrey
    1965   Death, Grief and Mourning, Garden City, New York:
            Doubleday & Co., Inc., (paperback).

Hadden, Jeffrey K. and Robert R. Evans
    1965   "Some Correlates of Religious Participation Among
            College Freshmen," Religious Education, Vol. 60,
            July-August, No. 4, pp. 277-285.

Hammond, Phillip E.
  1961   "Contemporary Protestant Ideology: A Typology of
          Church Images," Review of Religious Research,
          Vol. 2, (Spring), pp. 161-169.

Hardy, Kenneth R.
  1949   Construction and Validation of a Scale Measuring
          Attitudes Toward the L.D.S. Church, unpublished
          Master's Thesis, University of Utah.

Hepple, Lawrence M.
  1957   The Church in Rural Missouri, Part II, Religious
          Groups in Rural Missouri. Columbia, Missouri:
          A.E.S. Research Bulletin 633B, September, p. 63.

Herbert, Will
  1956   Protestant, Catholic, Jew, Garden City, New York:
          Doubleday & Co.

Hiemstra, William L.
  1966   "Self Perceptions and Perceptions of Selected Bible
          Characters: A Study of Depressed Psychiatric
          Patients," Religious Education, Vol. 61, January-
          February, No. 1, pp. 42-48.

Hood, Thomas C. and Kurt W. Back
  1967   "Patterns of Self-Disclosure and the Volunteer:
          The Decision to Participate in Small Group Experi-
          ments," paper presented at the meetings of the
          Southern Sociological Society, April.

Hutchinson, Russel S.
  1965   "A Study of Needs in Christian Adults," Religious
          Education, Vol. 60, September-October, No. 5,
          pp. 389-94.

Jones, Arthur Hosking
  1943   "Sex, Educational and Religious Influences on
          Moral Judgments Relative to the Family," American
          Sociological Review, 8, pp. 405-411.

Jones, Arthur R. and Lee Taylor
  1965   "Differential Recruitment of Female Professionals:
          A Case Study of Clergywomen," paper presented at
          the annual meeting of the Southern Sociological
          Society, Atlanta, Georgia, April, mimeographed,
          p. 5.

Jordan, Robert H.
  1955   "Social Functions of the Churches in Oakville,"
          Sociological and Social Research, Vol. 40 (November-
          December) pp. 107-111.

Jourard, Sidney M.
  1964   The Transparent Self, Princeton, N.J.: D. Van
          Nostrand Co., Inc.

Ketch, Clarence W. and J. David Lages
  1966   "Religious-Economic Survey of Springfield, Missouri,
          Springfield, Missouri: Southwest Missouri State
          College Press.

Krebs, Richard L.
  1970   "Roundup of Current Research," Transaction, Vol. 7,
          No. 5, (March), p. 8.

Kryvelev, I. A.
  1962   "Overcoming the Vestiges of Religion in the Lives
          of the Peoples of the USSR," (Moscow University,
          USSR), English Trans. of article in Soviet
          Anthropology and Archaeology, 1, 2, Fall, 11-21.

Lang, L. Wyatt
  1931   A Study of Conversion. London: George Allen and
          Undwin, Ltd., pp. 44-45. (Moberg)

Lazerwitz, Bernard
  1961   "Some Factors Associated with Variations in Church
          Attendance," Social Forces, Vol. 39 (May),
          pp. 301-309.

  1964   "Religion and Social Structure in the United
          States," 1964, in Religion, Culture, and Society,
          Louis Schneider, editor. John Wiley & Sons, Inc.,
          pp. 426-439.

Lenski, Gerhard
  1953   "Social Correlates of Religious Interest," American
          Sociological Review, Vol. 18, pp. 535-544.

Lindenfeld, Frank
  1960   "A Note on Social Mobility, Religiosity, and
          Students' Attitudes Toward Premarital Sexual
          Relations," American Sociological Review, Vol. 25,
          pp. 81-84.

London, Perry, Robert E. Schulman, and Michael S. Black
    1964   "Religion, Guilt, and Ethical Standards," Journal
            of Social Psychology, 63, pp. 145-159.

Lowenthal, Marjorie Fiske and Clayton Haven
    1968   "Interaction and Adaptation: Intimacy as a
            Critical Variable," American Sociological Review,
            Vol., 33, No. 1, February, pp. 20-30.

Luckmann, Thomas
    1967   The Invisible Religion, New York: The Macmillan
            Co.

Main, Earl D.
    1967   "Participation in Protestant Churches," Review of
            Religious Research, Spring, Vol. 8, No. 3,
            pp. 176-183.

Moberg, David O.
    1962   The Church as a Social Institution, New Jersey:
            Prentice-Hall, Inc., p. 256.

Moreton, F. E.
    1944   "Attitudes to Religion Among Adolescents and
            Adults," The British Journal of Educational
            Psychology, Vol. 2, Part 2 (June), pp. 69-79.

Mulford, Harold and W. W. Salisbury
    1968   "Self-Conceptions in a General Population, in
            Jerold Heiss (ed.) Family Roles and Interaction:
            An Anthology, Rand McNally and Company, Chicago,
            pp. 173-184.

Nash, Dennison and Peter Berger
    1962   "The Child, the Family and the 'Religious Revival'
            in Suburbia," Journal for the Scientific Study of
            Religion, Vol. II, No. 1, Fall, pp. 85-93.

O'Reilly, Charles T. and Edward J.
    1954   "Religious Beliefs of Catholic College Students
            and Their Attitudes Toward Minorities," Journal
            of Abnormal and Social Psychology, July, Vol. 49,
            No. 3, pp. 378-380.

Putney, Snell and Russel Middleton
    1961   "Dimensions and Correlates of Religious Ideologies,"
            Social Forces, Vol. 39, May, pp. 285-290.

Remmers, H. H. and D. D. Radler
  1962   "Teenagers' Attitudes Toward Study Habits, Voca-
          tional Plans, Religious Beliefs, and Luck," Report
          of Poll No. 67, The Purdue Opinion Panel, Lafayette,
          Indiana: Division of Educational Reference,
          December. (Taken from Bealer and Willets, 1967.)

Roucek, Joseph S.
  1966   "Special Characteristics of Religious Minorities
          in the U.S.," Indian Sociological Bulletin, Vol.
          IV, No. 1, October, pp. 55-64.

Ruppel, Howard J., Jr.
  1970   "Religiosity and Premarital Sexual Permissiveness:
          A Response to the Reiss-Heltsley and Broderick
          Debate." Journal of Marriage and the Family,
          7:647-655.

Salisbury, W. Seward
  1958   "Religion and Secularization," Social Forces, Vol.
          36, pp. 197-205.

Schofield, Michael
  1965   The Sexual Behavior of Young People, Little, Brown
          and Company.

Schommer, Cyril O., John Kosa, and Leo D. Rachiele
  1962   "Marriage, Career and Religiousness Among Catholic
          College Girls," Marriage and Family Living, 24/4,
          pp. 376-380.

Schuyler, Joseph B.
  1958   "Age and Sex Differentials in Religious Observance,"
          Proceedings of Fall Meeting, Society for the
          Scientific Study of Religion (October 31-
          November 1), pp. 10-11.

Semenfink, J. Anthony
  1958   "A Study of Some Aspects of Marital Behavior as
          Related to Religious Control," Marriage and Family
          Living, 20/2, pp. 63-169.

Siegman, Aron Wolfe
  1961   "An Empirical Investigation of the Psychoanalytic
          Theory of Religious Behavior," Journal for the
          Scientific Study of Religion, Vol. 1, pp. 74-78.

Sklare, Marshall
  1955   Conservative Judaism. Glencoe, Illinois: The
          Free Press, pp. 29, 53-54, 86-90.

Smith, T. Lynn
  1948   Population Analysis. New York: McGraw-Hill Book
          Company, pp. 186-188.

Sopher, David E.
  1967   "Geography of Religions," Prentice-Hall, Inc.,
          Englewood Cliffs, N.J.

Taggart, Morris
  1967   "Ecumenical Attitudes in the Evangelical Covenant
          Church of America," Review of. Religious Research,
          Fall, Vol. 9, No. 1, pp. 36-44.

Taves, Marvin J.
  1953   "Factors Influencing Personal Religion of Adults,"
          Washington Agricultural Experiment Station Bulle-
          tin 544, State College of Washington, Pullman,
          Washington.

Telford, C. W.
  1950   "A Study of Religious Attitudes," The Journal of
          Social Psychology, Vol. 31, pp. 217-230.

Turbeville, Gus
  1966   "Making Students Think," The Social Studies, Vol.
          57 (March) pp. 108-110.

Van Houtte, J.
  1964   "Urban Dominical Practice and Age in Western
          Europe," Archives de Sociologie des Religions,
          (University of St. Ignace, Antwerp, Belgium), 9,
          18, July-December, pp. 117-132.

Vernon, Glenn
  1956   "Background Factors Related to Church Orthodoxy,"
          Social Forces, Vol. 34, March, p. 252.

Vinacke, W. Edgar, Jan Eindhoven and James Engle
  1949   "Religious Attitudes of the Students at the Uni-
          versity of Hawaii," Journal of Psychology, Vol.
          28, pp. 161-179.

Walker, Charles R.
  1950   Steeltown. New York: Harper & Brothers, p. 44.

Wright, Derek and Edwin Cox
    1967   "A Study of the Relationship Between Moral Judg-
            ment and Religious Belief in a Sample of English
            Adolescents," The Journal of Social Psychology,
            72, 135-144.

Zetterberg, Hans
    1952   "The Religious Conversion as a Change of Social
            Rules," Sociology and Social Research, Vol. 36
            (January-February) pp. 159-166.

* Reprinted from Types and Dimensions of Religion, Glenn M.
  Vernon, ed., Salt Lake City: The Association for the
  Study of Religion, Inc., 1972, 103-132, with permission.

A FACTOR-ANALYTIC STUDY OF MALE-FEMALE DIFFERENCES IN MORMON RELIGIOSITY

J. D. Cardwell and D. B. Lindsey*

Among sociologists of religion, there is a widely accepted assumption that females are generally more religious than males. While there are research findings which support such an assumption, little direct attention has been given to isolating and explaining such difference. Thus, while research in the sociology of religion has taken male-female differences into account, little effort has been made to identify exceptions to the generalization that females tend to be more religious than males. In addition, no research has explored the question of whether female religiosity is different in either structure or content, or both, from male religiosity. In an earlier article dealing with male-female differences, Vernon and Cardwell (1972) pointed out that even when attention is called to this area in the literature it is usually limited in scope and frequently not well documented. In an effort to somewhat rectify the situation, this paper seeks to identify patterns which distinguish males and females through the analysis of the responses of 236 female and 344 male respondents who are members of The Church of Jesus Christ of Latter-day Saints. Our analysis of the

differences in male-female responses will explore such differences as they relate to the concept of religious commitment.

Religious commitment is a widely-used difficult concept
to define and is consequently, a difficult concept to research. Frequently, only one or two factors such as church
attendance and/or the belief of God are accepted as indicators of the more inclusive concept of religiosity. Recently, however, more sophistication has been introduced in
the area, with the notion of religiosity being conceptualized
as a general configuration which is defined by several substantive dimensions (Glock, 1962; King, 1967; Cardwell,
1971). Beyond this, however, there has been little in the
way of consistent research findings based on a multi-dimensional conception of religiosity. For example, the number
of possible dimensions has varied, based on reported research,
from five to more than twenty. As a result, the majority of
research available which has used the multi-dimensional
approach does not evidence a consistent definition of religiosity. However, if the structure or content of religious
commitment is different for males as opposed to females,
taking this phenomenon into account may aid the researcher
in arriving at more consistent results. This last possibility is an empirical question--an empirical question to
which this paper is directed.

Based on past research, it is clear that the over-all
pattern of religiosity is one of higher female than male
religiosity on the majority of the variables included.
Church attendance is often considered to be a measure of one
of the dimensions of religiosity. As would be expected, the
findings with reference to attendance support those concerning religiosity. When just church attendance is considered,
women tend to attend more regularly, and more frequently,
than do men. Although some surveys show a trend toward
equal attendance, no research (except some dealing with
Jewish and Mormon attendance) indicates that men attend more
frequently than females. It is known, however, that Catholic
men attend more frequently than Protestant men (Fichter,
1954).

These exceptions as regards attendance in particular are
also found with reference to religiosity in general. As
with attendance, the exceptions are the Jews (Argyle, 1959;
Bardis, 1964; Bemporad, 1966; and Lazerwitz, 1961) and the
Mormons (Cline and Richards, 1965; Hardy, 1949; and Vernon,

1956). This limited evidence is, of course, far from conclusive, but it does suggest that in these two groups the
pattern of higher female religiosity does not obtain. Rather,
evidence suggests that for these groups there is either higher
or equal male religiosity.

The distinctive patterns of male involvement for the Jews
and the Mormons may be related to the fact that each of these
church groups and their religious activities are male oriented. The role definitions of the church organizations
incorporate patterns of male superiority and female subordination. While individual, societal, and cosmic religion may
include such super-subordination beliefs, Church religion
reinforces the beliefs with organization and bureaucratic
interaction, in which such beliefs are given behavioral expressions. This increases the likelihood of male superiority
and the likelihood that males will exceed females in their
religious behavior.

In the Mormon church in particular, the priesthood is an
exclusive male phenomenon. Females are given important roles
to play in auxiliary organizations, but such roles and their
organization are clearly defined as auxiliary and, therefore,
of a different nature than the essential male organization.
There is no female clergy. It appears, therefore, that in
church religions where the role definitions specify high male
involvement, such involvement is higher than otherwise. If
this is a somewhat general pattern, most other research
apparently covers up this difference.

The Sample

The data for this study were collected from students who
were enrolled in a selected set of sociology classes and
attended class on a medium-size (student population approximately 25,000), state university in the Western United States.
Of the 580 students from whom data were collected, the majority (344) were males, and 236 were females. Only students
who identified themselves as members of The Church of Jesus
Christ of Latter-day Saints are included in this analysis.

Procedures[1]

A set of 32 Likert format items assumed in their totality
of reflect the five dimensions of religiosity suggested by
Glock (1962) were developed (see Table One for a more complete description of the items). All of the items have been

used in previous studies of religious commitment. (Faulkner and DeJong, 1966; Cardwell, 1969: Finner and Gamache, 1969; and Klemmack and Cardwell, 1971). Five of the items were assumed to reflect the religious belief or ideological dimension, and included such questions as "How strongly do you believe that Jesus is the Divine Son of God?" Another fourteen items were assumed to reflect the religious practice, or ritualistic dimension, and included such questions as "How frequently, in the last month, have you attended the regularly scheduled Sabbath worship services of your church?" The religious effects, or consequential dimension, was assessed by four items and asked such questions as "Is it morally acceptable for a Christian businessman, if he so desires, to keep his nonessential business open on Sunday?" Five additional items were assumed to reflect the religious experience dimension, and included such questions as "Have you ever had a sense of 'Union' with the Divine?" The final four items were assumed to reflect the religious knowledge, or intellectual dimension, and included such questions as "As far as I am concerned, the story of Genesis is literally true history."

A correlation matrix of the 33 items designed to measure the five dimensions of religious commitment was obtained for these Mormon respondents. Each of the matrices was then factored using a principal-components solution. Kaiser's criterion was used as an index of the completeness of factorization, and the resulting matrices were rotated to "meaningfulness" utilizing a varimax rotation (Harmon, 1967).

Results and Discussion

Examination of Tables One and Two indicates that important similarities exist among the two factor matrices. Both factor matrices appear to have several factors in common, although the order in which the factors appear varies from solution to solution. The factor matrices for both males and females are composed of five factors. While both groups produced five factors in factor analysis, they appear to have four factors in common. In general, the common dimensions can be identified as (I) religious ritualism, adult emphasis; (II) religious ritualism, youth emphasis; (III) religious belief; and (IV) religious experience. Each of the dimensions[2] has been previously identified in the general literature of the sociology of religion (Glock, 1962; Faulkner and DeJong, 1966; King, 1967; Klemmack and Cardwell, 1971).

TABLE I[3]

MALES

		II[a]	I	V	IV	III
BELIEF						
(10)	Belief[b]	.81	.13	.09	.14	-.02
(15)	Jesus	.82	.16	.31	.12	-.13
(20)	Bible	.50	-.09	.27	.16	-.10
(25)	Repent	.55	.21	.34	.33	-.01
(30)	Afterlife	.73	.17	.25	.20	.00
RITUALISM						
(1)	Fincon	.45	.37	.20	.55	.06
(2)	Ldrpos	.22	.34	.20	.09	.10
(3)	Sdact	.45	.43	.33	.47	.18
(4)	SSattd	.48	.40	.31	.48	.20
(5)	YGmbr	-.12	.84	.12	-.04	-.09
(7)	Chwrk	.36	.52	.30	.30	.17
(8)	Grace	.53	.27	.20	.40	.14
(9)	SDFrnds	.18	.49	.38	.38	.00
(17)	Rellit	.21	.22	.41	.22	.07
(22)	Weekattd	.42	.46	.30	.48	.20
(27)	Prayer	.73	.12	.18	.24	.09
(31)	Marige	.47	.20	.15	.52	-.07
(6)	YGattd	-.18	.86	.10	-.07	.11
EXPERIENCE						
(13)	Purpose	.31	.39	.46	.34	.07
(18)	Divine	.56	.28	.40	.11	.07
(21)	Truth	.30	.20	.47	.28	.31
(23)	Death	.30	.13	.44	.15	.08
(28)	Reason	.22	.06	.56	.41	.09
(32)	Faith	.28	.13	.62	.02	.02
KNOWLEDGE						
(1)	Geness	.37	.07	.14	-.59	.25
(12)	Rellif	.20	.29	.20	.18	.04
(16)	Mircal	.12	-.04	.12	.06	.55
(26)	Gospel	.12	.03	.12	.13	.69
EFFECTS						
(14)	Drink	.19	.26	.31	.41	.34
(19)	Polit	.11	.11	.07	.15	.04
(24)	Gamble	.21	.14	.48	-.44	.01
(29)	Divorce	.04	.01	.07	-.71	.10
(33)	Chrbus	.07	.17	.66	.10	.10

TABLE II[4]

FEMALES

		I[a]	V	III	II	IV
BELIEF						
(10)	Belief[b]	.71	.09	.33	.28	.13
(15)	Jesus	.70	.16	.32	.21	.10
(20)	Bibl3	.67	.01	.10	.03	.13
(25)	Repent	.33	.05	.70	.31	.07
(30)	Afterlife	.60	.10	.55	.13	-.04
RITUALISM						
(1)	Fincon	.31	.17	.30	.64	.18
(2)	Ldrpos	-.08	.23	.20	.62	.02
(3)	Sdact	.29	.28	.34	.63	.16
(4)	SSattd	.23	.17	.24	.81	.15
(5)	YGmbr	-.14	.78	-.14	-.36	.07
(7)	Chwrk	.27	.47	.29	.35	.03
(8)	Grace	.43	.14	.25	.38	.02
(9)	SDFrnds	.13	.16	.12	.38	.39
(17)	REllit	.01	.45	.05	.16	.26
(22)	Weekattd	.24	.28	.25	.67	.23
(27)	Prayer	.68	.11	.36	.32	.06
(31)	Marige	.38	.24	.63	.12	.03
(6)	YGattd	-.12	.85	-.19	-.28	.06
EXPERIENCE						
(13)	Purpose	.11	.17	.66	.20	.21
(18)	Divine	.37	.34	.34	.05	.17
(21)	Truth	.31	.38	.40	.25	.34
(23)	Death	-.02	.14	.68	.20	.03
(28)	Reason	.24	.14	.60	.23	.16
(32)	Faith	.17	.07	.81	.09	.08
KNOWLEDGE						
(11)	Geness	.52	.25	.29	.05	.46
(12)	Rellif	.09	.40	.28	.02	.49
(16)	Mircal	.13	.02	.02	.03	.11
(26)	Gospel	.22	.06	.11	.25	.08
EFFECTS						
(14)	Drink	.17	.24	.34	.27	.61
(19)	Polit	.08	.05	.01	.10	.14
(24)	Gamble	.02	.25	.42	.30	.42
(29)	Divorce	.00	.16	.17	.17	.19
(33)	Chrbus	.14	.11	.25	.25	.41

All five of the religious belief items for the male and four of the five belief items for the female respondents have substantial loadings on the religious belief factor (factor two for males and factor one for females). In addition, items which were assumed to reflect other dimensions of religious commitment also load on the belief factor for both males and females. However, the critical factor in considering this dimension is not how many items load for any given group, but on which _factors_ the items load. The belief items have substantial loadings on the belief factor for both groups and _do not have substantial loadings on any other factors_. Thus, it appears that both male and female Mormon respondents share fairly parallel belief factors.

Although communalities in the belief factor exist for both groups, there are also striking dissimilarities. For example, an examination of the items assumed to measure other dimensions load on the belief factor for both males and females. However, eight items for males, as opposed to only three items for females, also define the belief factor, even though they are from different dimensions. This outcome would suggest that religious belief is more broadly conceived for the Mormon males than for Mormon females.[5] Such findings regarding the belief factor and other dimensions as well, can be attributed in large measure to the unique authority structure of the Mormon church. In addition to the authority structure, the formal norm-role definitions associated therewith, must also be considered. In both instances, structure and norm-role definitions are primarily prescriptions reflecting official church doctrine which becomes an important factor to consider when studying Mormon behavior.[6]

As previously indicated, the priesthood is an exclusive male phenomenon which constitutes the dominant authority structure within the Mormon church. The priesthood organization is composed of eight distinct "offices" or positions. Each office is hierarchically located with strictly delineated lines of power and authority including rather clearly prescribed roles which direct the activities of an incumbant's priesthood office. The Mormon priesthood is further divided on the basis of a "higher" and "lower" order; i.e., the Melchizdek Priesthood and the Aaronic Priesthood. These two distinctions can be further characterized roughly in terms of focal concerns wherein the Melchizdek Priesthood has more to do "with things spiritual" and the Aaronic Priesthood has more to do "with things temporal," regarding church operations and affairs.

117

All other organizations within the church structure in which operational control is given to women (such as the Women's Relief Society or the Primary Children's Association), remain subordinate to, and under the general supervision of, a priesthood authority. For Mormons, there is no power or authority to officiate except as delegated by and through the "power" of the priesthood. This rule also holds for "all other authorities or offices in the church....," and such are considered only as "appendages to (the) priesthood." (McConkie, 1958:432).

To illustrate, Deacons, the lowest ranking office in the Mormon priesthood come under the direction of the Ward Bishop to assist him in temporal matters.[7] For example, they may be called upon to collect money (Fast Offerings) by canvassing ward members' homes on a monthly basis or engage in various assignments related to the care and maintenance of the local church building and grounds or other properties such as welfare farms and other enterprises wherein unskilled labor can be utilized. Deacons also assist in distributing the church's sacrament to the congregation during Sunday worship services." If required, Deacons assist Teachers, the next higher priesthood rank, and are to generally "watch over the church." Twelve Deacons comprise a quorum which is presided over by a president and two counselors selected from within its membership.[8]

About age 14, young males are usually called to be Teachers. Their duties under the Ward Bishop are to "warn, expound, exhort, and teach, and invite all to come unto Christ." Such duties are normally fulfilled under the direct supervision of an adult male companion who is a member of the Melchizedek priesthood, while conducting monthly visits to local ward members' homes. Teachers quorums are composed of 24 members, presided over by a president and two counselors which is normally the structuring found in all priesthood organizations.[9]

About age 16, many Mormon youths, if they are considered worthy, are "called" to be Priests. Priests are to "preach, teach, expound the scriptures, baptize, administer the Sacrament, and visit the house of each member, and exhort them to pray vocally and in secret and attend to all family duties." In addition, the Priest "may also ordain other Priests, Teachers and Deacons." "And he is to take the lead of meetings when there is no Elder present." Quorums are composed of 48 members under the presidency of the Ward Bishop.[10]

118

The next upward step is being "called" and ordained to the Melchizedek Priesthood as an Elder. Frequently this occurs when males reach the age of 19 or 20 and are called to serve on two-year, full-time proselyting missions. Such missions are served at the personal financial expense of those "called." Frequently, however, costs are supplemented by families, friends, and in some cases by donations raised through the individual's Priesthood Quorum. Mission calls may be within the United States or to foreign countries. Other male youths may be required to wait until they have reached majority to attain this office, or until they are considered ready to take on the responsibilities of a family and marriage. That is, in order to marry within the church, (Temple Marriage) a prerequisite is to hold the office of Elder.

Specifically, the duties of Elders (besides preaching the Gospel at home and abroad) are to administer all the ordinances of the church and engage in any or all duties prescribed for Deacons, Teachers, and Priests as required. Ninety-six Elders comprise a quorum presided over by the usual presidency.[11]

With no specific tenure in "office" as an Elder or age specifications, Elders may be "called" to become a Seventy. However, such calls usually come only after one has demon-strated some church-related "ability" and greater "maturity" as determined by the various higher authorities. Seventies are considered travelling ministers and are especially or-dained to preach the Gospel. It is not entirely unusual or unexpected for men "called" to this position to be "called" on a second full-time mission. More often, however, they act as part-time local missionaries proselyting within the bounds of their local ward or stake.[12] Seventy members com-prise a seventies quorum; however, Seventies are presided over by seven presidents selected from within their member-ship.[13]

If a male member has demonstrated "ability" and "maturity" and is considered worthy, if he is not "called" to become a Seventy, he is most likely "called" to be a High Priest. These office holders are to officiate in all ordinances and blessings of the church. High Priest quorums are found in all Stakes of the church. There is no limit on quorum member-ship and it is presided over by a president and two counselors. Generally, from the ranks of the High Priests most top leader-ship positions are recruited such as Bishops, Stake Presidents, and their counselors.[14]

The next higher step in the Melchizedek Priesthood is that

of a Patriarch. Few reach this position as this "office" is
limited in numbers. Usually there is one Patriarch per
State or in other districts of the church. Patriarch's pro-
nounce blessings on church members and declare their lineage.
There is only one Patriarch of the church, a position which
is assumed by lineage (father to son) and he is considered
one of the general authorities of the church. The incum-
bent of this office is under the direction of "Quorum of the
Twelve" (12 "Mormon" Apostles) which in turn acts under the
direction of the First Presidency of the Church.[15]

Apostles constitute the highest "calling" in the church
and act as special witnesses for Christ in the world. They
are to build, organize and administrate the church wherever
possible in the world. Twelve Apostles form a quorum with
its senior member acting as President of that Quorum. It is
church tradition that the senior member of this Quorum succeed to the office of the President of the church upon the
death or other possible loss of the Church President.[16]

Supervision over the entire Mormon church is the task of
the First Presidency, normally consisting of the President
and two counselors. These three men are responsible to conduct all matters of policy, organization and administration.
The church President is considered by Mormons to be a prophet,
seer and revelator for the whole church and thus guided by
direct revelation and inspiration from God.[17]

Constituting the group known as the General Authorities
of the church are the Patriarch of the Church, the First
Quorum of seventy, comprised of the Seven Presidents of
Seventy, the Quorum of the 12, the Presiding Bishopric and
their designated assistants and counselors. (McConkie,
1958). Under various General Authorities are the heads of
the general auxiliaries and general boards consisting of
specialists to assist in the planning, operations, and
administration of all church activities.[18]

As can be seen, Mormon males who are actively involved in
church affairs operate within relatively clear-cut parameters.
For the upwardly mobile, each office offers considerable re-
inforcement and reward in terms of recognition, power,
authority, and prestige. For the "true" believers come
additional satisfactions in the "concrete" belief that one
is achieving and working towards the highest rewards of
Mormonism--not merely salvation, but exaltation in the
Celestial Kingdom of God, the highest of many degrees of

glory in the after life.

As a general rule, in order to advance within the priesthood, minimal standards of behavior prescribed by the church
must be met. Herein we are able to more specifically de-
scribe and account for the differences found between male
and female commitment beginning first with the youth ritualism dimension.

Youth Ritualism Factor

The importance of youth ritualism for males becomes readily apparent by taking into account the nature and extent of
the priesthood duties just described and the social processes
associated with such duties in addition to other factors
which will be accounted for later in this investigation.

For example, prior to being interviewed by his Ward
Bishop for entry into the Priesthood, the young LDS male
typically undergoes a lengthy period of church preparation
and socialization in the Primary Association. Primary is an
organization which holds weekly meetings that include periods
of formal instruction. Many LDS children between the ages
of 8 to 12 attend these meetings which usually follow the
school day. "The Primary (Association) operates units in
all the wards and branches of the Church. For Proselyting
purposes primaries are often organized by missionaries without reference to other church organizations. Children are
graduated from the primary organizations to the Mutual
Improvement organizations and the priesthood quorums."
(McConkie, 1958:540). During the primary years considerable
emphasis is placed on learning Church history and lore as
well as basic principles of Church doctrine.[19]

Within all church organizations, however, considerable
emphasis is placed on teaching and learning. Parentheti-
cally, one factor which should be noted, is the pervasive-
ness with which male dominance is entertained throughout all
such teaching. Exemplifying this practice, John Widtsoe, a
prominent Mormon general authority, now deceased, in his
writings on Priesthood and Church Government, explains the
patriarchal order and organization of the Mormon family in
this way:

The Father is Spokesman and Leader. The family, a
group of intelligent beings, must be organized, else
chaos results. Just as there is but one Priesthood,

121

but many offices in it, so every member of the family circle has equal claims upon the blessings of the home, but is assigned different tasks in connection with family life.

There must be a presiding authority in the family. The father is the head, or president, or spokesman of the family. This arrangement is of divine origin. It also conforms to physical and physiological laws under which humanity lives. A home, as viewed by the Church, is composed of a family group, so organized as to be presided over by the father, under the authority and the spirit of the Priesthood conferred upon him. (Porter, 1963:349-350)

And, the not atypical reaction of submissiveness demonstrated by female members of the Mormon Church is aptly illustrated by Katheryn Lau Tanner's remarks written for the Improvement Era, a widely-read church periodical:

When I read and hear all these facts about the Priesthood, I feel very humble and grateful to have at the head of my house a man who has been worthy to be ordained an elder in the Holy Melchizedek Priesthood.....Although we cannot actually hold the priesthood, we can share in the blessings of it with and through our husbands; it is our responsibility to help and support them in every way.....A man who honors his priesthood is entitled to wisdom and inspiration from his Heavenly Father; so I feel that when I go to my husband for advice and counsel, I can depend on him to give me counsel that is sound and good and to help me when there is a difficult decision to make .....(Porter, 1963:346-347)

Thus, we can proceed to further clarify how, through the emphasis on male dominance, such dominance becomes a salient factor in determining male-female differences regarding religious commitment among Mormons.

Upon entry into the Aaronic Priesthood, each male is interviewed by an authority to insure he is "living the gospel." Although, at earlier stages of advancement such interviews may be somewhat perfunctory, with each succeeding move upward, interviews tend to become more inquisitorial. That is, are you paying a full tithing (10% of one's gross income)? Are you keeping the Word of Wisdom (no smoking,

122

drinking, coffee, tea or other harmful habits)?[20] Are you
keeping the law of chastity and in general living a clean
moral life? The prerequisites of "worthiness" for entry
into the Melchizedek Priesthood outlined in the Mormon
Church's General Handbook of Instructions, (1968:78) involve
the following:

1. Have sincere faith in the restored gospel of Jesus
   Christ, and in the mission of the Prophet Joseph
   Smith, and sustain the President of the Church as
   the living prophet of God, and other general and
   local authorities in their respective callings.

2. Have no affiliation, in sympathy or otherwise, with
   any of the apostate groups or individuals who are
   running counter to the accepted rules and doctrines
   of the Church.

3. Desire to use their talents, means, and abilities
   in building up the kingdom of God and spreading the
   gospel in the earth.

4. Be morally clean, honest, prayerful and otherwise
   fit to receive priesthood ordination.

5. Observe the Word of Wisdom.

6. Be willing to strive earnestly to do their duty
   in the Church, to live in accordance with its rules
   and doctrines, to pay a full tithing, attend
   sacrament, priesthood, and other meetings, and to
   be active in priesthood affairs.

It is further emphasized that the "Brethern should prove
themselves worthy before they are ordained." Unsatisfactory
answers to any of these questions may delay or preclude
upward mobility in the church until the Ward Bishop or other
concerned authority is satisfied there is sufficient indica-
tion of repentance and compliance.[21]

Thus, for those young Mormon males who reach age 12 and
are beyond their primary socialization and enter into
priesthood activity, a second phase of youth-oriented activity begins. Both males and females may continue on in
Mutual Improvement Association activities wherein expectations and opportunities for their ritualistic behavior are
comparable in many respects. Considering first, however,

the opportunity and expectations for such behavior in males, it increases with the added responsibilities "Priesthood bearers" may assume, and which appears to be the most significant influence affecting male commitment.

For example, males are expected to attend weekly priesthood meetings which are normally held early Sunday mornings. It is during these meetings, in addition to periods of classroom instruction, that many special assignments involving both temporal and secular duties are made. All such assignments include duties at Ward and/or Stake levels of jurisdiction. These assignments as stated earlier, may include anything as mundane as maintenance of church grounds and buildings to assisting in the construction of new buildings to working on special welfare projects such as farms and in canneries, to taking an active part in ritualistic ceremonies, while teaching, preaching, or otherwise instructing church members or potential church converts in a variety of contexts.

In addition, the Mormon Church, which prides itself on its record keeping function, considering it of "tremendous importance," maintains records and statistics on many such activities at both individual and group levels. (McConkie, 1958:559). Competition is not an unusual result and may become keen between either individuals and/or groups of youths for honors regarding the fulfillment of these assignments. An important feature of these activities is that young males are thus provided with objective criteria whereby they become more "visible" and following those presiding over them, their peers and they themselves are enabled to take note of and distinguish "appropriate" behavior and thereby respond accordingly. These salient aspects, it can be observed, tend to become even more pronounced and influential in neighborhoods and areas which are predominantly populated by those of the Mormon faith.

A third important aspect to consider in accounting for the youth ritualism dimension, indicated earlier, is the Mutual Improvement Association (MIA). The MIA is the Mormon Church's youth organization and this church auxiliary is intended to meet the needs of Mormon youth ranging in age from 12 through about 30. Further, the MIA is divided on the basis of young men and young women's organizations; however, a number of joint activities are coordinated between the two organizations.

Each organization is further divided into smaller groups

where activities are tailored to coincide with the varying
interests related to age and maturity. For males, this
includes a complete program of Boy Scouting activites as
well as athletic competition. The young women accordingly
have their counterparts and in addition there are programs
for young married couples.

The Mormon Church in placing a heavy emphasis in
"wholesome" activity, considers such activity "is an essential and vital part of the gospel of salvation-- a gospel
which makes provisions for every need of man, both temporal
and spiritual." (McConkie, 1958:559) MIA activity includes,
"parties, banquets, dinners, games, athletic endeavors, and
contests, dramas, dances, concerts, radio and television
programs, picnics, outings, camping trips, and hunting and
fishing trips...." MIA meetings are usually held weekday
nights, during the early evening hours. However, in addition
to the many "secular" activities, extensive classroom instruction preaching or other modes of gospel teaching are integrated into many of the varied activities.

More importantly, however, in terms of the development
of a religious commitment concerning youth ritualism, especially the male dimension, there remains the factor of male
dominance. Male "headship" is consistently emphasized and
supported via the leadership function of the priesthood with
its attendant authority, power and prestige.

Thus, it can be seen how youth ritualism becomes an important factor in the lives of LDS youths but especially for
LDS males, as it is the youth ritualism which appears first
in order for them. First, during their primary years, Mormon
males are "trained up" in the preparation to assume priesthood duties and to continue on in other church related
activities and organizations. Secondly, upon ordination to
the Aaronic Priesthood, they are expected to pursue an extensive course of active participation. Such participation
involves, assuming a dominant leadership role when attending
to Priesthood, Sunday School and Sacrament Meetings on Sundays. While on Sundays and other days of the week there
are additional periods of time taken to fulfill an assort-
ment of church related assignments of either a "temporal" or
"secular" nature. Thirdly, consideration must be given the
expected weekly attendance and involvement in connection with
youth oriented programs sponsored by the Mutual Improvement
Association, which activity can be considered as merely an
uninterrupted extension of their "primary" activities.

Examination of the data shows that it is precisely those considerations involved within the three major contexts just mentioned, which load on and define the youth ritualism dimension for LDS males.

Additionally, it can be seen that individual males are frequently brought together in a host of church related activity.[22] This activity combined with the church's extensive record keeping function which involves formal and informal competition and rewards, makes it a relatively easy task to "keep track" of where one stands. That is, developing the availability of a number of objective criteria. Added to such criteria is the frame of reference which one may develop as inactive members are frequently sought out and systematically "worked with" in order to "restore" them. Therefore, we are able to account for the two additional items defining the youth ritualism factor for LDS males-- self definitions of one's activeness and that of friends.

In general, it should be further stated regarding these findings that the Mormon Church provides highly organized and structured programs for all of its membership. For those who choose to participate, but particularly males, they are required to operate within relatively narrow, doctrinally prescribed bounds. Those who violate church proscriptions often find it difficult to continue active church participation. For example, violation of the "Word of Wisdom" (smoking, consumption of alcohol, tea or coffee, etc.) is apt to be emphatically noted and called to their attention and negatively sanctioned and if the "sinner" is not directly dealt with, negative sanctions may accrue in a variety of subtle but unmistakable ways.

First, deviants are not likely to be advanced upward through the priesthood ranks and are thus, effectively, excluded from a number of group associations and activity. Secondly, perceived "good" which is objectively recorded on the basis of some minimal level active participation is supported through a formal and informal system of personal rewards and public recognition; such rewards are unlikely to be forthcoming to those perceived as not "good."

In short, youth ritualism is a salient factor involved in the LDS male's religious commitment wherein norm-role definitions and expectations for behavior entail much more than a passive nominal acceptance of the faith.

126

Whereas youth ritualism was the first factor extracted for males, it was the last factor solution produced for females. Nevertheless, as a factor common to both, the similarities and differences can be accounted for within the same conceptual framework as was male commitment. That is, on the basis of the norm-role definitions, expectations of others for certain kinds of religious behavior including doctrinal prescriptions and the authority structure of the Mormon Church.

First, women may not hold the priesthood and cannot participate in the variety, nor with the same frequency as males, ritualistic behavior. For example, in the relatively few instances when females may be "called" to become full-time missionaries; although they may in fact be the ones to convert a new member to the Mormon Church, they are without authority to perform any of the church's ritualistic cere-monies connected with making such conversions "official," e.g., baptism and the "laying on of hands for the gift of the Holy Ghost."

Nevertheless, females are generally expected to partici-pate in church work and frequently do. However, all female positions and work assignments are under the general super-vision of the priesthood authority. Although the positions held and the formalized work accomplished by females is considered important and is recognized, generally it does not assume the same preeminence afforded priesthood functions or functionaries. In addition, most of the major positions for females tend to be filled more often by older adult women. Thus, youthful female activity in matters of church meetings is more often restricted to passive attendance rather than active participation. Therefore, it does not appear as imperative for women to emphasize church atten-dance rather than active participation. Therefore, it does not appear as imperative for women to emphasize church attendance in the same manner as men. In this same regard, definitions of activity of self and friends do not become such an important focal concern as is the case with males.

The data show that reading of religious literature is an item extracted for females only, which further defines the youth ritualism dimensions for them. Such a finding is not unexpected however, if we take into account differences which can be found in the content prescribing female-male role activity, particularly in regard to MIA activities. That is, while males may be engaged in scouting activities, athletic events and other activities characteristically

127

associated with maleness, females are more likely to engage in the study of the social and educational aspects of religion involving such things as "ethics" or morals, "biography," "art," "music," history or practical religion. Thus, it can be seen how the reading of religious (Mormon) literature can assume greater importance involving youthful female ritualism.

Secondly, most of the official church activity women engage in other than a few leadership positions normally involve teaching positions for the instruction of younger children. This, of course, also involves the additional reading of religious literature in preparing their lessons. We cannot be as certain in attempting to account for why leading a religious life becomes an important item extracted for females and not males in the youth ritualism dimension. It seems, however, that this finding is closely associated with the orientation prevalent in the Mormon Church, that a young woman's primary task is to grow up preparing to assume certain duties which are in a sense considered as important as the male's priesthood duties. That is, females are primarily expected to prepare for a "proper" church marriage and to assume the "sacred" duties of motherhood. Full realization of such is, of course, at least threatened unless one lives a religious life in order to gain entry into an LDS Temple for the purpose of marriage. Expressing this general viewpoint, Kathryn Lau Tanner writes:

This division of responsibility is for a wise and noble purpose. Our Father in Heaven has bestowed upon His daughters a gift of equal importance and power, which gift, if exercised in its fullness, will occupy their entire life on earth so that they can have no possible longing for that which they do not possess. The "gift" referred to is that of motherhood--the noblest, most soul-satisfying of all earthly experiences. If this power is exercised righteously, woman has no time nor desire for anything greater, for there is nothing greater on earth! This does not mean that women may not use to the full their special gifts, for they are possessed of human free agency to the same extent as are men. Also, the more woman exercises her innate qualifications the greater is her power for motherhood. Woman may claim other activity, but motherhood should take precedence in her entire scheme of life.

.....The gift and responsibilities of motherhood make it desirable that women should be freed from the obligations of active service in the Priesthood. A

fair and wise adjustment has been made by the Lord,
so that women have the freedom from unnecessary Church
responsibility in order to magnify their great calling
as mothers of men. (Porter, 1963:352)

Last, it can be found that considerable emphasis is
placed on the females' church defined role throughout their
MIA careers. Hence, it is on the same basis described here
that a number of male-female differences in Mormon religiosity can be explained in addition to the youth ritualism
dimension.

To review the findings thus far, LDS males and females
share fairly parallel belief factors. Strikingly, however,
religious belief appears more broadly conceived for males
than females. The most apparent explanation for this phenomenon arises out of the fact that the Mormon Church places
heavy emphasis upon a service orientation and particularly
in the case of its male membership.

Further evidence indicating that the forcefulness with
which service is put forth leads to an apparent integra-
tion of activity/ritualism and belief, in terms of "church"
expectations is clearly reflected in statements made by all
LDS Church "Prophets." However, no clearer examples can be
found than those provided by the often quoted Brigham Young,
second President of the Mormon Church, and Joseph Fielding
Smith, a recently deceased President of the Church, who was
noted for his doctrinal and historical sophistication in
church matters. First, however, to explain factor loadings
common to both males and females involving the belief dimension, we need to look no further than the most basic statement of Mormon belief which summarizes the fundamental
tenants of the Mormon religion--The (13) Articles of Faith,
as set forth by Joseph Smith, founder of the Mormon Church:

1. We believe in God, the Eternal Father, and in His
    son, Jesus Christ, and in the Holy Ghost.

2. We believe that men will be punished for their own
    sins, and not for Adam's transgression.

3. We believe that through the Atonement of Christ,
    all mankind may be saved, by obedience to the laws
    and ordinances of the Gospel.

4. We believe that the first principles and ordinances

of the Gospel are: first, Faith in the Lord Jesus Christ; second, Repentance; third, Baptism by immersion for the remission of sins; fourth, laying on of hands for the gift of the Holy Ghost.

5. We believe that a man must be called of God, by prophecy, and by the laying on of hands, by those who are in authority to preach the Gospel and administer in the ordinances thereof.

6. We believe in the same organization that existed in the Primitive Church, vi., apostles, prophets, pastors, teachers, evangelists, etc.

7. We believe in the gift of tongues, prophecy, revelation, visions, healing, interpretation of tongues, etc.

8. We believe the Bible to be the word of God as far as it is translated correctly; we also believe the Book of Mormon to be the word of God.

9. We believe all that God has revealed, all that He does now reveal, and we believe that he will yet reveal many great and important things pertaining to the Kingdom of God.

10. We believe in the literal gathering of Israel and in the restoration of the Ten Tribes; that Zion will be built upon this (the American) continent; that Christ will reign personally upon the earth; and, that the earth will be renewed and receive its paradisiacal glory.

11. We claim the privilege of worshipping Almighty God according to the dictates of our own conscience, and allow all men the same privilege, let them worship how, where, or what they may.

12. We believe in being subject to kings, presidents, rulers, and magistrates, in obeying, honoring, and sustaining the law.

13. We believe in being honest, true, chaste, benevolent virtuous, and in doing good to all men; indeed, we may say that we follow the admonition of Paul - We believe all things, we hope all things, we have endured many things, and hope to

130

be able to endure all things. If there is anything
virtuous, lovely, or of good report or praiseworthy,
we seek after these things.

Returning to our earlier point, the biblical administion
referring to "faith and works" found in James, 2:14-26
which is taken quite literally by Mormons is clearly and
unequivocally translated into an important facet of Mormon
religious behavior and is exemplified in the admonitions of
both Young and Smith. Early in church history, Young maintained that "true Believer" needs qualifying for many believe but do not obey. The only true believers are those
who prove their belief by their obedience to the requirements of the Gospel.[23]

Reiteration of Young's early admonition is seen in the
doctrinaire statements of Smith (1956:149;150;153) who
writes:

Membership in the Church is not for the idler. He who
seeks an easy road to salvation must go elsewhere, it
is not to be obtained in the Church.....

When a man confesses that it is hard to keep the
commandments of the Lord he is making a sad confes-
sion--that he is a violator of the Gospel Law.....

The Father does not intend that the members of the
Church shall sit down and wait for the Kingdom of
God! He has said:

"Thou shall not be idle; for he that is idle
shall not eat the bread nor wear the garments
of the laborer.---D.C. 42:42.

Let every man be diligent in all things. And
the idler shall not have place in the church,
except he repent and mend his ways--Ibid. 75:29."

The man who does only those things in the Church which
concern himself alone, will never reach exaltation.
For instance, the man who is willing to pay his tithes
and offerings, and to attend to the ordinary duties
which concern his own personal life and nothing more,
will never reach the goal of perfection....be given
in behalf of others.

131

As can be seen in the data, the belief dimension is heavily loaded with ritualism items denoting the service orientation and requires "active" membership which is integrated closely with what one's beliefs are, that is, if they are to be defined as "true believers." Many Mormons who believe, but are "luke warm" and fail to adequately or appropriately demonstrate or prove their belief often acquire the popularly used label of "Jack" Mormon.

The single item defining this dimension for LDS males which is neither a ritualism or belief item is an experiential item—a sense of "union with the divine." This finding is not entirely surprising nor inconsistent with Mormon belief and practice however. When one is acting in God's name and believes his actions are directed by God via several possible forms of revelation the idea should become clear. That is, Mormon teaching is replete with the doctrine that members of the church can literally receive revelation from God to help direct them in their personal lives; however, such dogma is especially important regarding the conduct of church related affairs insofar as one's particular office is concerned and insofar as a revelation is not contrary to "official" church doctrine, policy, or the revelations of higher authorities. (McConkie, 1958:579-586) Thus, if a person so believes and then perceives that whatever church activity he works at is at least acceptable by his own standards and those of the presiding authority, he may define such interest, enthusiasm or dedication as divine revelation or inspiration and hence, a sense of "union" with the divine.[24] In fact, McConkie (1958:582) asserts for Mormons or anyone else for that matter there is "NO SALVATION WITHOUT REVELATION.----"

Therefore, within the LDS context of a strong belief-service orientation and the expectations which serve to structure activities and behavior, Mormon males appear to adopt a broad, conceived belief structure which is also experienced in the manner described.

Religious Knowledge

The religious knowledge dimension constituted one of two dimensions which were found to be uncommon factors defining religious commitment among LDS males and females. The religious knowledge dimension was produced only in the case of LDS males. Sufficiently high factor loadings which defined this dimension were found in only three, but nonetheless important instances. They were: time spent reading religious literature, belief in the miracles of the Bible and that they were caused by God setting aside natural law, and the number of the first four gospels correctly identified.

For Mormon males, knowledge of a theological nature is considered an indispensable commodity, much more so than for females. And, again, these results are primarily seen to arise out of the LDS male's priesthood functions and responsibilities already enumerated. Emphasizing the point further, however, we find that the Mormon Church's position and one's commitment to it wherein knowledge is concerned, involves a peculiar, if not interesting relationship. In the beliefs and teachings of the LDS Church, it is maintained that without the priesthood there can be no authority to act in God's name, (an imperative) nor is there any "real" knowledge of God to be had without the power of the priesthood. (Smith, 1956:210-217) More clearly stating the case for Mormons, McConkie (1958:388-389) writes:

> Gospel knowledge deals primarily with a clear perception of the truths about God and His laws....All types of knowledge however, are not of equal worth.... Knowledge of the arts and sciences--of mathematics, chemistry, history, medicine, and the like have no bearing whatever on attainment of salvation. It is the knowledge of God and His laws that leads to high reward in the hereafter....But the saints are expected to specialize in the knowledge of the truth, the knowledge that makes known the mysteries of the kingdom and the wonders of eternity....

Regarding these issues, McConkie (1958:459) further elaborates by citing numerous instances in which miracles are found throughout Mormon holy literature and notes: that these miracles are "typical" among those found in the "true" church, "indeed," even "common." Thus, our findings seem explained within this context, because it is a basic Mormon belief that the "keys" and "power" to knowledge and various other courses of action (i.e., "minor" miracles at least) reside within the "restored" priesthood and those who bear its authority to act in God's name.

In order for Mormons to acquire their theological knowledge, it requires the study and reading of considerable religious literature. In fact, they are not only encouraged to read, and study, but in the Doctrine and Covenants they

133

are indeed commanded to read and study the "best" and the "good" books. It becomes immediately apparent to any who become even somewhat familiar with Mormonism that great stress is placed on the extent to which Mormons are expected to become involved with their religious literature. Indeed, one needs only to observe the amounts and variety of religious literature carried to and from an LDS Priesthood meeting or Sunday School meeting to become aware of their emphasis upon the acquisition and use of religious literature. Therefore, for LDS males, reading and gaining the special knowledge required of them is a highly important factor in the maintenance of their religious activities and responsibilities and which differs markedly from the expectations concerned with most LDS females.[25]

These findings thus provide us with a strong explanation for the difference found between males and females regarding the religious knowledge dimension. In addition, such findings are consistent within the content of church structure, authority, norm-role definitions and expectations for LDS male-female behavior.

Adult Ritualism

Adult ritualism factors were extracted for both LDS males and females. However, the data show that this dimension is more simply defined for females than for males. That is, 11 items factored out for males as opposed to five for females.

There are four ritualism items both males and females have in common; these factors, it seems, can be considered as merely an extension or carry over of expectations and behavior from youthful activity with the exception of a concern for financial contributions. The appearance of a financial contribution item as a part of adult ritualism dimension can logically be viewed as developing in conjunction with one's concern and involvement in an "adult world" wherein making and spending money is a more pronounced concern in the case for most young people.

That is, for persons reaching 18 years of age, many are just entering the job market and considering careers which obviously involves considerations of financial rewards. And for many females, although they may not enter a job market, they are, of course, frequently involved with matters of family finances which come with marriage.

134

For adult Mormons the matter of financial contributions is of no little concern. All are expected to give freely of their "increase" to a variety of church related funds, especially as it regards the matter of the law of tithing, which is emphasized about as much as any other church doctrine. That is, all Mormons are expected, indeed commanded, to contribute 10% of their gross earnings or "increase" to the Church coffers.[26]

In addition to tithing, there are assessments made or contributions expected to such items as the Ward budgets, Stake budgets, Building Funds, monthly Fast Offerings, Missionary Support Funds and Welfare donations of varying types. Recalling the prerequisites for advancement in the priesthood or for obtaining permission to enter one of their temples (and in many cases permission to engage in other active positions), it can be seen that the paying of financial obligations is a salient factor in LDS religious commitment. Although the youth of the LDS Church are also expected and taught to donate freely, expectations for their actual behavior in this regard are not as a rule nearly so high nor involved as is the case with adult Mormons.

The fifth and last item which defines adult ritualism for females, is seen to involve leadership positions. For males, it will be recalled, this item appears as an earlier factor in their commitment involving youth ritualism. For LDS females, however, we would expect such a factor to develop later within their church activity and tenure. That is, for those females over 18 years of age there is generally greater opportunity to assume leadership positions because that is the approximate age when females can become active Relief Society members or they are considered qualified to assume adult leadership positions with the women's MIA organization. Also, the opportunity to teach or lead in the children's Primary Association with various Sunday School classes or secretarial positions generally increases with age. However, with recent church changes involving restructuring of the MIA, it's quite possible these findings will shift for females and thus become an aspect of their youth ritualism dimension.

Additional ritualism items defining the adult ritualism dimension for LDS males include saying grace with meals and a belief that marriage should be performed by an authorized church official. The importance of these two factors can be attributed to that of male concern with assuming leadership role dictated by their Priesthood requisites.

For example, in the case of saying grace with meals, not only is the adult Mormon male likely to take part in this ritual regularly, but he is also most likely to direct other members of his family as to when they will take their turn at saying grace.

In addition, during one of the family mealtimes when most of the family would be present the occasion for saying grace may become a more solemn ritual than merely praying over the meal. That is, it may be a time when many LDS adult males "take the lead" in holding family prayer--a greatly encouraged ritual for LDS families. For example:

"It is the counsel of the Church that family prayer should take place twice daily, ordinarily before the morning and evening meals. Where there are several members of a family, and particularly where children are involved, these family prayers should not include the blessing on the food; such should be a separate prayer, offered as the family sits around the table and after they have risen from their knees in connection with the more formal and extended prayer. There would be no impropriety, however, in a man and his wife alone (there being then no children who need the training and experience involved) to include the blessing on the food in the formal family prayer."
(McConkie, 1958:526)

That the appropriate type of marriage ritual is a salient aspect of a LDS male's commitment and especially for the highly committed adult appears to need no further explanation; however, such is not the case for LDS females wherein marriage is an item which defines their religious experience.

The remaining items regarding adult ritualism for males do not admit of straightforward interpretation. However, it seems plausible that in the course of male involvement with the "everyday" affairs of Ward, Stake, or other Church business and decision making regarding "sacred" matters which are intimately involved with affairs that are of a more "profane" nature (such as who is "worthy" to do this or that because of what they are, or are not doing relative to drinking, gambling, etc.), these items become salient relative to adult male activity. Whatever explanation is advanced for these loadings, it remains that behavior relative to drinking, divorce, and so forth, is religiously defined for Mormon males.

Religious Experience

Religious experience was the last factor extracted for males and the third for females. The experience factor is highly parallel for both groups. The common experience dimension can, therefore, be assessed in a very general way in terms of the literalness with which Mormons view their capabilities for religious experience relative to their concrete, well-defined, and all encompassing view of Mormon doctrines of salvation and exaltation - males and females differing cnly in regard to afterlife and marriage, and religious literature and divine for men.

With respect to the two uncommon items for females, they probably reflect the idealistic and romantically conceptualized Mormon idea of marriage with the Mormon emphasis on marriage in the afterlife thrown in. Thus females experience in a similar way the two notions of marriage and afterlife.

Regarding the items common to males only (religious literature and divine) these loadings have probably already been explained in terms of knowledge and power relative to priesthood responsibility as this is translated into a divine experience or a sense of union with the divine.

Religious Effects

That only females defined an effects dimension is consistent with repeated findings in the sociology of religion that males tend to "know" their religion and females tend to "practice" it (Fukuyama, 1960). It is interesting to note that only one effects item (Gambling) loads on any other factor in the matrix for females. It is also interesting to note that of the three effects items which define this factor for females, each revolves around behaviors that have been specifically prohibited by the Word of Wisdom and/or the Gospel Doctrine. It is not surprising, therefore, that two of the knowledge items also loaded on this female factor. The two items from the religious knowledge scale appear to refer to knowledge or "truth" as it is defined by the institutional church, i.e., that Genesis is literally true history (.46) and that a truly religious life is dependent on following the doctrine of the institutional church (.49).

Essentially, therefore, factor four for females is defined as an effects factor within the framework of acceptable secular behavior set forth by the institutional church.

Summary

The differences in the pattern of loadings between the two groups can be conceived of as a function of differing theological emphases within Mormonism as they are communicated to lay individuals. Mormon males probably respond to belief items from a different set than Mormon females. In any case, belief is confounded with other dimensions of religiosity for Mormon males.

The critical point of this article resides in the comparability of multidimensional measures of commitment between sexes. The results indicate, at least in a tentative sense, that the particular manifestation of each dimension of commitment varies between the sexes. Belief for Mormon males is not the same as belief for Mormon females because the items assumed to measure belief for males are confounded with ritualism. Apparently the Mormon male, when considering belief, also considers its relationship to ritualism. Similar results were obtained for the remaining dimensions.

It seems unreasonable to assume that the various dimensions of religiosity are equivalent between sexes within denominations.[27] All religious groups emphasize some aspects of religiosity for one sex more than the other, giving those emphasized a broader, richer meaning. Naturally, important similarities exist between sexes, and it is critical to isolate these as well. However, such similarities are problematic and the researcher, rather than assuming a parallel structure of religiosity between sexes, would be well advised to demonstrate it empirically.

FOOTNOTES AND REFERENCES

* Reprinted from Measuring Mormonism, Vol. 1, (April) 1974, 1-26, with permission.

1. Copies of the complete questionnaire are available from the authors upon request.

2. As far as we know, the youth ritualism dimension was initially isolated in Cardwell and Klemmack (1971).

3. Supra-script a denotes that roman numeral refers to the
    order in which the factor appears in the rotated solu-
    tion. For convenience, the factors are reordered in
    the following manner: Belief, youth ritualism, experi-
    ence, adult ritualism, knowledge.
    Supra-script b denotes that the number at the start of
    each item refers to the order in which the item appears
    in the religiosity section of the questionnaire.

4. Supra-script a denotes that roman numeral refers to the
    order in which the factor appears in the rotated solu-
    tion. For convenience, the factors are reordered in
    the following manner: Belief, youth ritualism, experi-
    ence, adult ritualism, effects.
    Supra-script b denotes that the number at the start of
    each item refers to the order in which the item appears
    in the religiosity section of the questionnaire.

5. Breadth of a factor here refers simply to the number of
    different items having high loadings on a given factor.
    A high breadth factor is one on which many items have
    high loadings, while a low breadth factor is one on
    which few items have high loadings.

6. For Mormons, this means directly revealed or ordered by
    divine revelation from God to "the Prophet" (Church
    President) living on earth. These revelations are com-
    piled as Mormon scripture, they are considered holy and
    can be found in the Doctrine and Covenants, which is
    further broken down by section and verse. For example,
    D. & C. 107:1-4.

7. A ward is equivalent to a local parish and the Ward
    Bishop is the presiding priesthood authority, a High
    Priest in the Melchizedek priesthood comparable to a
    local pastor or minister of a parish.

8. See for example: D. & C. 20:57; 84:111; 107:85.

9. See for example: D. & C. 20:59; 107:86.

10. See for example: D. & C. 20:46-47; 107:87-88.

11. See for example: D. & C. 20:16; 38, 45, 61, 81, 107:89.

12. Several wards within a geographical area form a stake,
    an area similar to a diocese.

13. See for example: D. & C. 107:10.

14. See for example: D. & C. 107:10.

15. See for example: D. & C. 107:39-50; 124:123-128.

16. See for example: D. & C. 107:23, 39, 58; 124:127-128.

17. See for example: D. & C. 102:23, 39, 58; 124:124-126.

18. See for example: D. & C. 124:91-94; 123-124.

19. Emphasis added; however, such is not a necessary rite of passage.

20. The Word of Wisdom is the health law of the Church stressing that which is prohibited and that which is encouraged; however, the negative proscriptions seem most frequently emphasized. See: D. & C. 89:1-21.

21. Female members also must submit to such interrogation when applying for a "Temple Recommend," i.e., permission for entry into a Temple.

22. In addition to the other factors mentioned, the formation of relatively stable group membership is enhanced inasmuch as it is unusual for ward members to attend or become active in other than their own geographically prescribed ward. Church authorities are reticent to transfer membership records except in extraordinary circumstances. Such records also act as recommendations without which full participation in church affairs is not permitted.

23. Emphasis added. Brigham Young may well be the most instrumental figure in Mormon history to firmly establish and set the precedent in matters of church policy which is still followed today. See for example, any of the 26 volumes of The Journal of Discourses published under the auspice of the LDS Church, particularly Volume I, regarding many such statements.

24. This is not to deny that some or even many Mormons experience various phenomena referred to by some as "altered states of consciousness" which involves dreams, imagery or other sensory perceptions and which may indeed have religious content. See for example: Charles T. Tart

(ed.) <u>Altered States of Consciousness</u>, 1969.

25. For example, the focus on female reading offered in the 1972-73 Relief Society Manual featured six lectures in each of the following areas: Homemaking, Cultural Refinement, Spiritual Living, and Social Relations.

26. See for example, Sec. 119, D. & C.

27. In an earlier article Klemmack and Cardwell (1973) suggested that the structure of commitment varies between denominations.

Argyle, Michael
1959 <u>Religious Behavior</u>. Glencoe, Ill.: Free Press, pp. 71-79.

Bardis, Panos D.
1964 "Religiosity Among Jewish Students in a Metropolitan Community," <u>Sociology and Social Research</u>, Vol. 49, No. 1 (October), pp. 90-96.

Bemparad, Jack, Rabbi
1966 "Some Effects of Intermarriage on Children," in Zurotsky, Jack J., ed. <u>The Psychological Implications of Intermarriage</u>.

Cardwell, Jerry D.
1969 "The Relationship Between Religious Commitment and Attitudes Toward Premarital Sexual Permissiveness: A 5-D Analysis," <u>Sociological Analysis</u> (Summer), 30, 2, 72-80.

1971 "Multidimensional Measures of Interfaith Commitment: A Research Note," <u>Pacific Sociological Review</u> (January), 14, 1, 79-88.

Cline, V. B. and J. M. Richards, Jr.
1965 "A Factor-Analytic Study of Religious Belief and Behavior," <u>Journal of Personality and Social Psychology</u>, 1, 569-578.

Faulkner, J. E. and G. F. DeJong
1966 "Religiosity in 5-D: An Empirical Analysis," <u>Social Forces</u>, (December) 45, 246-254.

Fichter, Joseph H.
1954 <u>Social Relations in the Urban Parish</u>. University of

Finner, S. L. and J. D. Gamache
   1969 "The Relation Between Religious Commitment and
         Attitudes Toward Induced Abortion," _Sociological
         Analysis_, 30 (Spring), 1-12

Glock, C. Y.
   1962 "On the Study of Religious Commitment," _Religious
         Education_ (Research Supplement) July-August, S98-
         S110.

Hardy, Kenneth K.
   1949 "Construction and Validation of a Scale Measuring
         Attitude Toward the L.D.S. Church," unpublished
         Master's thesis, University of Utah, Salt Lake City,
         Utah.

Harmon, Harry H.
   1967 _Modern Factor Analysis_. Chicago: University of
         Chicago Press.

Klemmack, D. L. and J. D. Cardwell
   1973 "Interfaith Comparison of Multidimensional Measures
         of Religiosity," _Pacific Sociological Review_
         (October), 16, 4, pp. 495-507.

Lazerwitz, Bernard
   1961 "Some Factors Associated with Variations in Church
         Attendance," _Social Forces_, (May) 39, 301-309.

McConkie, Bruce R.
   1958 _Mormon Doctrine_, 2nd ed. Salt Lake City: Bookcraft,
         Inc.

Porter, Blaine R.
   1963 _Selected Readings in the Latter-Day Saint Family_,
         Dubuque, Iowa: Wm. C. Brown Co.

Smith, Joseph Fielding
   1956 "The Way to Perfection," Geneological Society of the
         Church of Jesus Christ of Latter-Day Saints, Salt
         Lake City, 2nd ed.

Vernon, Glenn M.
   1956 "Background Factors Related to Church Orthodoxy,"
         Social Forces, 34 (March), 252.

Vernon, G. M. and J. D. Cardwell
  1972 "Males, Females, and Religion," in Types and
        Dimensions of Religion. Salt Lake City: Assn. For
        the Study of Religion, Inc.

General Handbook of Instructions: the Church of Jesus Christ
of Latter-Day Saints, Number 20, 1968. Published by the
First Presidency of the Church of Jesus Christ of Latter-Day
Saints.

ON KEEPING THE SABBATH DAY HOLY: PERCEIVED POWERLESSNESS AND
CHURCH ATTENDANCE OF MORMON MALES AND FEMALES*

Jerry D. Cardwell

The research reported herein concerns the relationship between church attendance and perceived powerlessness within
the institutional church. The rationale for investigating
the possible relationships between perceived powerlessness
and church attendance is attendant on the position of several
sociological scholars that the institutional church is under-
going changes which when viewed from the framework of traditional religious institutions, are defined as undesirable.
Reference is made, for example, to empirical studies by Glock
and Stark (1965) and Glock (1968) which suggest that American
society is witnessing a decline of traditional church religion (Vernon, 1972) as an important institution, and to the
theoretical statement of Thomas Luckmann (1967) which arrives
at a similar conclusion by suggesting that traditional religion is moving to the periphery of society.

The suggestion that traditional religion is declining in
American society brings to mind several interesting hypotheses. It is possible, for example, that participation in
traditional church religion declines as perceived powerlessness on the part of church parishioners increases. If such
were found to be the case, such data would suggest that the
well documented decrease in participation in church religion

may be occurring concomitant with a perceived inability to personally affect the institutional church.

Conceptual Framework

Michael Smith (1971) has suggested that alienation-- as manifest in a sense of powerlessness-- is characteristic of many facets of life in large, complex urban centers. He also suggests that "the sheer size and anonymity of urban life help(s) to produce generalized feelings of powerlessness in the face of large-scale institutions." This perceived diminished ability to affect institutions may lead to estrangement from such institutions and the larger society as well. Although dealing specifically with urban public service bureaucracies, Smith's comments have strong relevance for religious institutions in contemporary, urban America. According to Smith:

> Unlike factories and corporations, the professed goal of urban public services bureaucracies is helping people rather than selling products. Alienation is likely to become particularly acute among the workers or unorganized clients of such bureaucracies when persons rather than things are the goals likely to be displaced by impersonal routinized practices, by excessive specialization of function, or by prolonged clientele dependence.

Smith's (1971) thesis is easily translated, without loss of relevance, to religious bureaucracies in a straightforward manner. For example, there can be little argument that a professed goal of religious institutions is one of helping people. In view of such parallels it is reasonable to suggest that the powerlessness dimension of alienation is likely to be prevalent among those parishioners who constitute the unorganized laity if and when such groups perceive that decision making within the church bureaucracy is impersonal, highly rountinized, and not responsive to individual preferences of the unorganized laity.

From the several efforts to clarify the concept of alienation has come the suggest to view the relationship between the various dimensions of alienation as a process. Such a view has been proposed by Browning, Farmer, Kirk, and Mitchell (1961):

> We propose that the concept of alienation be

146

regarded as consisting of three stages of development which we will call: (1) the predisposing stage, (2) the stage of cultural disaffection (Browning, Farmer, Kirk, and Mitchell, 1961), and (3) the stage of social isolation.

The predisposing stage is inclusive of three of the categories developed by Seeman (1959), and occur in the following sequence: powerlessness, meaninglessness, and normlessness. In this scheme, a sense of powerlessness is cognitively prior to one of meaninglessness, and as Browning has suggested, "when an actor's means-ends scheme is no longer meaningful, he ceases to feel that the normative structure is binding upon him (normlessness). One consequence of this state of normlessness is the decision to cease adaptative behavior and subsequently withdrawal from the institutional structure (1961)." The position this paper takes is that Seeman's process can be applied to participation within the institutional church and, therefore, that perceived powerlessness is a salient factor in the individual's decision to cease attendance at the regularly scheduled Sabbath worship services of the institutional church. Thus, one relationship to be explained in this research is that between perceived powerlessness and church attendance. The expectation is that perceived powerlessness activates the predisposing stage of alienation and will be inversely related to church attendance.

The Sample

In order to assess the hypothesis that participation in traditional church religion declines as perceived powerlessness increases, data were collected from students who attended a large (student population approximately 25,000) state university in the Rocky Mountain area of the United States. Of the 320 students from whom data were collected, 133 were female and 187 were male. All of the respondents used in this study provided a religious self definition of themselves as "very religious." All of the respondents used in this study were members of the Church of Jesus Christ of Latter-day Saints (mormons).

Methods

A set of 9 Likert-format items assumed to measure three dimensions of perceived powerlessness within the institutional church were derived. The items were designed to measure

147

perceived powerlessness relative to the individual's perceived ability to influence "others," "lay leaders," and the "minister," to make decisions about "issues," "social issues" and "religious issues," that are of concern to the respondent. For example, a typical religious issues question would ask: "Do you think you can influence the minister of your church to take a stand on religious issues (such as prayer in the school) that concern you?" Possible responses were yes, probably yes, probably no, and no.[1] Number of sabbath worship services attended in the past month is used as the measure of church attendance. Responses to the attendance and powerlessness items are correlated using Yule's Q and the Chi-square test of independence is used as a test of significance.

Results and Discussion

The initial hypothesis regarding the relationship between church attendance and perceived powerlessness is supported for each of the nine powerlessness items. The zero-order associations (Q) between church attendance and perceived powerlessness range from moderately negative (Q = -.35) to very strong negative (Q = -.83).[2] Assuming that the attendance variable is antecedent to the perception of powerlessness, one explanation of these general findings is that perception of powerlessness initiates the process of withdrawal from the institutional church.

More specifically, however, this research is concerned with male-female differences (if any) in church attendance with regard to perceived powerlessness. In other words, given that church attendance and perceived powerlessness are negatively associated, is it possible that sex is a salient factor in the specification of that general relationship. Stated differently, the Q values that represent the relationship between church attendance and perceived powerlessness may be significantly different between sexes, suggesting that the strength of the relationship between the independent and dependent variables varies with sex.

Apparently, sex has no influence on the relationship between perceived powerlessness in the general category of "issues" or the more specific category of "social issues" and church attendance. When the relationship between these powerlessness variables and church attendance is controlled by sex, no significant difference is noted between the Q values for the different sexes. However, this is not the case when the

relationship between perceived powerlessness on religious
issues and church attendance varies with sex of the
respondent.

TABLE 1

Do you think you do not have enough voice about your Church's
stand on religious issues (such as prayer in the school) that
concern you?

Church Attendance (% high) and Perceived Powerlessness, Controlling for Sex of Respondent

| Sex | Percent High on Church Attendance | | |
| | Perceived Powerlessness | | |
	Low	High	% Diff.
Male	62.7 (110)	53.2 (77)	9.5
Female	87.3 (71)	58.1 (62)	29.2

Q (Males) = -.19
Q (Females) = -.66 x^2 = 6.179, p. $<$ .025.

As indicated in Tables 1 through 3, the general relationship between perceived powerlessness on religious issues and
church attendance is specified by the control variable sex.
That is, powerlessness has a very strong negative correlation
with church attendance for females (Q = -.66) when the source
of the powerlessness is unspecified. The negative correlation
for males is a low negative association (Q = -.19), and the
difference between the two correlations is significant at the
.025 level (Table 1). A similar relationship obtains in Tables
2 and 3 with the notable exception that males are most affected
when the source of the perceived powerlessness is specified,
i.e., the minister or lay leaders.

TABLE 2

Do you think you can influence the minister of your Church to take a stand on religious issues (such as prayer in the school) that concern you?

Church Attendance (% high) and Perceived Powerlessness, Controlling for Sex of Respondent

Sex	Percent High on Church Attendance		
	Perceived Powerlessness		
	Low	High	% Diff.
Male	78.2 (87)	42.0 (100)	36.2
Female	75.6 (82)	70.6 (51)	5.0

Q (Males) = -.66
Q (Females) = -.13 x^2 = 6.072, p. $<$ .025

To summarize the findings thus far, perceived powerlessness and church attendance are negatively correlated across all powerlessness items. When sex is introduced as a control variable, the relationship between the independent and dependent variables are unaffected when the perceived powerlessness is relative to the general category of "issues" or the more specific category of "social issues." However, sex does appear to be an important variable in specifying the relationship between perceived powerlessness and church attendance when the perceived powerlessness is relative to the response category of "religious issues." An examination of the data concerning religious issues indicates that when the source of the perceived powerlessness is undefined, the perception of powerlessness has a far greater impact on female attendance than on male attendance. However, when the source of the perception of powerlessness is defined, the impact on attendance is greater for male parishioners than for females. One

150

explanation of these differences can be found in the norm-role definitions characteristic of the Mormon Church bureaucracy.

TABLE 3

Do you think you can influence the lay leaders in your Church to take a stand on religious issues (such as prayer in the school) that are important to you?

Church Attendance (% high) and Perceived Powerlessness, Controlling for Sex of Respondent

Sex	Percent High on Cnurch Attendance		
	Perceived Powerlessness		
	Low	High	% Diff.
Male	84.5 (71)	43.1 (116)	41.4
Female	80.0 (65)	67.6 (68)	12.4

Q (Males) = -.76
Q (Females) = -.31 x^2 = 4.929, p. $<$ .05

Based on past research, it is clear that the over-all pattern of religiosity is one of higher female than male religiosity on the majority of the variables measured (Vernon and Cardwell, 1972). Church attendance is often considered to be a measure of religiosity and, as would be expected, the findings with reference to attendance support those concerning religiosity. When just church attendance is considered, women tend to attend more regularly, and more frequently, than do men. Although some surveys show a trend toward equal attendance, no research (except some dealing with Jewish and Mormon attendance) indicates that men attend more frequently than females. It is known, however, that Catholic men attend more frequently than Protestant men (Fichter, 1954).

These exceptions as regards attendance in particular are also found with reference to religiosity in general. As with attendance, the exceptions are the Jews (Argyle, 1959; Bardis, 1964; Bemporad, 1966; and Lazerwitz, 1961) and the Mormons (Cline and Richards, 1965; Hardy, 1949; and Vernon, 1956). This limited evidence is, of course, far from conclusive, but it does suggest that in these two groups the pattern of higher female attendance does not obtain. Rather, evidence suggests that for these groups there is either higher or equal male attendance.

The distinctive patterns of male involvement for the Jews and the Mormons may be related to the fact that each of these church groups and their religious activities are male oriented. The role definitions of the church bureaucracies incorporate patterns of male superiority and female subordination, and reinforce the beliefs with organizational and bureaucratic interaction in which such beliefs are given behavioral expression.

In the Mormon church in particular, the priesthood is exclusively a male phenomenon. Females are given important roles to play in auxiliary organizations, but such roles and their location in the organization are clearly defined as auxiliary and, therefore, of a different nature than the essentially male organization. This increases the likelihood of male superiority and the likelihood that males will exceed females in church attendance.

An examination of the data in Table 1 suggests that for those Mormon females who are affected by a general sense of powerlessness (the source of the powerlessness is not role specific), such a perception activates the predisposing stage of alienation which then has important implications for the frequency of church attendance. These results seem clearly consistent within the context of the authority structure of the Mormon church bureaucracy. That is, while Mormon females are generally expected to participate in the church and frequently do, all female positions and work assignments are under the general supervision of the priesthood authority. Although the positions held and the formalized work accomplished by females is considered important and is recognized, it does not assume the same preeminence afforded priesthood functions. In addition, most of the major positions for females tend to be filled often by older adult women. Thus, youthful female activity in matters of church meetings is typically restricted to passive attendance rather than active participation. These data suggest that if the expectation for passive attendance is perceived as a sense of powerlessness, Mormon females will withdraw their attendance from church meetings.

Tables 2 and 3 indicate results which suggest that male attendance is affected when the perceived powerlessness is relative to a specific role or role set. It is interesting to note that role specific perceived powerlessness appears to have little effect on female attendance. Again, these results can be accounted for in terms of the bureaucratic authority structure of the Mormon church. As previously indicated, the priesthood is an exclusively male phenomenon and constitutes the dominant authority structure within the Mormon ward.[3] Thus, Tables 2 and 3 report data which measure the individual's perceived ability (or lack of it) to affect those in authority positions with close proximity to those he occupies.

In general, it can be stated that the Mormon church provides highly organized and structured programs for all of its membership. For those who choose to participate, but particularly for males, they are required to operate within relatively narrow, doctrinally prescribed bounds. For those males who are not normatively advanced upward through the priesthood ranks and are, therefore, effectively excluded from a number of group associations and activities, it is often difficult to continue active church participation. One explanation is that perceived powerlessness within the dominant authority structure of the local ward may be a salient factor in activating the predisposing stage of alienation for Mormon males.

Summary

On the basis of these data it is suggested that perceived powerlessness is operative in the specification of attendance at regularly scheduled Sabbath worship services (in the Mormon church). It appears that both the nature and the source of the perceived powerlessness have important implications for attendance.

These data also seem to suggest several implications. Apparently, a sense of powerlessness or power is related to structural considerations. Because the character of an organization may not appear the same to all of its members (even when they occupy the same general level within it), Mormon men who believe that they should have "specific power" to influence the minister or lay leader may withdraw attendance when they perceive that they lack such ability. In contrast, Mormon women have little reason to believe that they can, or should, be able to influence their minister or lay leader and are minimally disturbed (as measured by church attendance) when it is confirmed that they indeed lack this ability. However, when the Mormon female finds that the "diffuse power" which she believes to be her just right is denied, she may respond by withdrawing her attendance. Thus, the expectations about legitimate influence and the beliefs about personal circumstances seem to be critical elements in producing a sense of powerlessness. It is clear that the mere absence of power means little when one does not expect to possess that power.

Neither Mormon men or women respond in an alienated manner to the absence of power to influence "issues" or "social issues." It would seem to be a legitimate speculation that a change in belief is associated with a changed perception of power/powerlessness even though the social situation of the actor has not altered. The three components of beliefs, objective opportunities, and organizational structure interrelate to produce a variety of outcomes.

Another implication concerns the special vulnerability of the female respondents to what might be called "situational alientation." They are college students and presumedly imbued with some measure of the American female's sense of significance. Her church offers some opportunity for participation and influence although it is quite limited when contrasted with the situation in some other denominations of a similar ideology (e.g., Southern Baptists). Their passive attendance seems incongruous with the expectations they hold about legitimate influence. While one can only speculate, it would be instructuve to compare these respondents with less extensively educated Mormon women of the same age. Another possibility for instructive comparison would be with a group of extensively educated, but older Mormon women who have had greater opportunity to acquire positions of influence more consistent with their expectations.

FOOTNOTES AND REFERENCES CITED

*Paper accepted for publication in a forthcoming issue of the Virginia Social Science Journal. Used with permission.

1. For purposes of the utilization of the "words" and 2X2X2 program, the responses to the independent variable were

collapsed by combining the "yes" and "p/yes" responses and the "no" and "p/no" responses into low and high powerlessness respectively. Church attendance was collapsed into high (2 or more times in past month) and low (zero or 1 time in past month)categories.

2. Description of the magnitude of the Q values is taken from Davis (1971, 49). A complete list of all of the zero-order Q's is available from the author on request.

3. A Ward is equivalent to a local parish and the Ward Bishop is the presiding priesthood authority, a High Priest in the Mechizedek priesthood comparable to a local pastor or minister of a parish.

Argyle, Michael
    1959 Religious Behavior. Glencoe Ill., Free Press, pp. 71-79.

Bardis, Panos D.
    1964 "Religiosity Among Jewish Students in a Metropolitan Community," Sociology and Social Research, Vol. 49, No. 1, (October), pp. 90-96.

Bemporad, Jack, Rabbi
    1966 "Some Effects of Intermarriage on Children," in Zurotsky, J. J., ed., The Psychological Implications of Marriage, New York: Supreme Printing Co., Inc.

Browning, Charles and others
    1961 "On the Meaning of Alienation," American Sociological Review,26, 5, October.

Cline, V.B. and J.M. Richards
    1965 "A Factor-Analytic Study of Religious Beliefs and Behavior," Journal of Personality and Social Psychology," 1, 569-578.

Davis, James A.
    1971 Elementary Survey Analysis. Englewood Cliffs, N.J.: Prentice-Hall, Inc., p. 49.

Fichter, Joseph H.
    1954 Social Relations in the Urban Parish. University of Chicago Press, 61, 91-93.

Glock, C.Y. and R. Stark
    1965 Religion and Society in Tension. Chicago. Rand-McNally.

Hardy, Kenneth K.
    1949 "Construction and validation of a scale measuring attitude toward the L.D.S. Church," unpublished M.A. thesis, University of Utah, Salt Lake City, Utah.

Lazerwitz, Bernard
    1961 "Some Factors Associated with Variations in Church Attendance," _Social Forces_, (May) 39, 301-309.

Luckmann, Thomas
    1967 _The Invisible Religion_. New York. Macmillan Company.

Stark, Rodney and C.Y. Glock
    1968 _American Piety_. Berkeley. University of Calif. Press.

Seeman, Melvin
    1959 "On the Meaning of Alienation," _American Sociological Review_, 24, No. 6, December, 784-790.

Smith, Michael P.
    1971 "Alienation and Bureaucracy: The Role of Participatory Administration," _Public Administration Review_, (Nov/Dec), 658-664.

Vernon, G. M. and J. D. Cardwell
    1972 "Males, Females, and Religion," in _Types and Dimensions of Religion_. Salt Lake City: Association for the Study of Religion.

Vernon, G. M.
    1972 "Types of Religion: Religion in 4-T," in _Types and Dimensions of Religion_. Salt Lake City: Association for the Study of Religion.